THE END
OF THE
COLD WAR

CHRISTINE HATT

WORLD ALMANAC® LIBRARY

Please visit our web site at: www.worldalmanaclibrary.com
For a free color catalog describing World Almanac® Library's
list of high-quality books and multimedia programs,
call 1-800-848-2928 or fax your request to (414) 332-3567.

Library of Congress Cataloging-in-Publication Data

Hatt, Christine.
  The end of the Cold War / by Christine Hatt.
    p. cm. — (The Cold War)
  Includes bibliographical references and index.
  Summary: Explores why the Cold War ended, including such reasons as the changing relationship between the United States and the Soviet Union, economic problems, and the increase in nuclear weaponry worldwide.
  ISBN 0-8368-5275-3 (lib. bdg.)
  ISBN 0-8368-5280-X (softcover)
  1. Cold War—Juvenile literature. 2. United States—Foreign relations—Soviet Union—Juvenile literature. 3. Soviet Union—Foreign relations—United States—Juvenile literature. 4. Post-communism—Juvenile literature. 5. Nuclear warfare—Juvenile literature. 6. World politics—1945—Juvenile literature. [1. Cold War. 2. United States—Foreign relations—Soviet Union. 3. Soviet Union—Foreign relations—United States. 4. Post-communism. 5. Nuclear warfare. 6. World politics—1945-.] I. Title. II. Series.
  D843.H357   2002
  327.73047—dc21   2001046648

This North American edition first published in 2002 by
World Almanac® Library
330 West Olive Street, Suite 100
Milwaukee, WI 53212 USA

This U.S. edition © 2002 by World Almanac® Library. Original edition published in Great Britain in 2002 by Hodder Wayland, a division of Hodder Children's Books. Additional end matter © 2002 by World Almanac® Library.

Series concept: Alex Woolf
Editor: Joanna Bentley
Designer: Derek Lee
Consultant: Scott Lucas, Head of American and Canadian Studies, University of Birmingham
Map illustrator: Nick Hawken
World Almanac® Library designer: Scott M. Krall
World Almanac® Library editor: Jim Mezzanotte
World Almanac® Library production: Susan Ashley and Jessica L. Yanke

Picture credits: Associated Press: 18, 39; Corbis/© Peter Turnley: 32; Polfoto: 13, 33; Popperfoto: 4, 6, 7, 8, 9, 11, 14, 15, 19, 24, 27 (top), 28, 29, 34, 36, 37, 40, 45, 46, 47, 49, 52, 54, 56, 57, 58; Topham Picturepoint: 12, 16, 20, 27 (bottom), 41, 42, 44, 50, 55; United Nations: 31; Wayland Picture Library: 5

Quotation sources: *The White House Years* by Henry Kissinger (Weidenfeld & Nicolson, 1979); *Memoirs* by Mikhail Gorbachev (Doubleday, 1996); *Jugement à Moscou. Un Dissident dans les Archives du Kremlin* by Vladimir Boukovsky (Robert Laffont, 1995); *The Moscow Summit, 1988: Reagan & Gorbachev in Negotiation* by Joseph Whelan (Boulder, Westview, 1990); *At the Highest Levels: The Inside Story of the End of the Cold War* by Michael Beschloss and Strobe Talbott (Little Brown, 1993); *Washington Post* (September 28, 1991); *The Cold War, An International History 1947-1991* by S. J. Ball (Arnold/Hodder Headline, 1998)

Printed in the United States of America

1 2 3 4 5 6 7 8 9 06 05 04 03 02

Contents

CHAPTER ONE

Changing Times

By 1976, the Cold War was showing no signs of ending. Born in the aftermath of World War II, the Cold War had been based on a rivalry between the world's two superpowers, the United States and the Soviet Union. Each had its own set of allies, and each sought to support its own ideology — capitalist democracy in the case of the United States, communism in the case of the Soviet Union — in various parts of the world. This rivalry prompted massive arms buildups by both nations and drove conflicts in Korea, Vietnam, and elsewhere.

Yet in the first half of the 1970s the Cold War became dramatically less frosty. Pursuing a policy of *détente*, which means a loosening of tensions, U.S. and Soviet leaders sought to improve relations and reduce the possibility of nuclear war.

NIXON AND KISSINGER

This change in the Cold War was due in large part to the initiatives of U.S. president Richard Nixon, a Republican who took office in 1969. Foreign policy was Nixon's specialty. With the assistance of Henry Kissinger, who was the president's national security adviser and then, in 1973, U.S. secretary of state, Nixon worked to thaw the icy U.S.-Soviet relationship.

PROBLEMS AND SOLUTIONS

When Nixon came to power, the United States faced two major foreign-policy problems. The first was the country's deep and troubled involvement in Vietnam. U.S. troops, fighting on behalf of non-communist South Vietnam against the communist, Soviet-supported forces of North Vietnam, were dying in the thousands. American public opinion had largely turned against U.S. involvement in the conflict, and many Americans wanted Nixon to end the bloodshed. The second problem was the Soviet nuclear arms buildup. In the 1960s, the Soviet Union's stockpile of nuclear weapons had grown so

President Nixon (right) and Henry Kissinger pursued a complex foreign policy that combined assertion of U.S. strength with pursuit of détente.

rapidly that it now matched U.S. nuclear capability.

Nixon and Kissinger both believed that the best solution to these two problems was to draw closer to the Soviets. The Soviet government would be invaluable in persuading North Vietnam to end the war, and the Soviet Union's cooperation would also be necessary if the spiraling arms race was to be controlled.

The Soviets had their own practical reasons for wanting détente. Soviet military spending had reached dizzying new heights, but industrial development, especially in high-technology fields such as computing, lagged far behind the West's. The Soviets believed that a limited reconciliation with the United States would ease pressure on its weak economy, while opening up the possibility of importing Western goods and technological expertise.

▲ U.S. involvement in Vietnam began in the 1950s, escalated dramatically during the 1960s, and came to a bitter and unsuccessful end in 1973. For both sides of the conflict, the cost in terms of suffering and loss of life was immense.

NEW RELATIONS WITH CHINA

Nixon and Kissinger adopted a twin-track approach. In November 1969, they began arms control negotiations with the Soviets. Known as the Strategic Arms Limitation Talks (SALT), the negotiations proceeded at an infuriatingly slow pace. At the same time, the United States made overtures to China, the world's other great communist power.

The main purpose in seeking out China was to unsettle the Soviets, who had originally been staunch allies of the Chinese but had fallen out with them over policy differences. In 1969, a violent border dispute only increased hostility between the two countries. The Soviets were wary of China's growing power, which was now bolstered by nuclear weapons. Nixon visited Beijing in February 1972. For the Soviet Union, the prospect of its two enemies forming an alliance was horrifying.

SALT I

As Nixon and Kissinger had hoped, friendlier relations between the United States and China jolted the Soviets into moving forward with the SALT talks. Just three months after his visit to Beijing, Nixon flew to Moscow, where he and Soviet premier Leonid Brezhnev signed the SALT I agreement on May 26, 1972. It placed a limit of 200 antiballistic missiles (ABMs) on both superpowers and introduced a five-year freeze on the production of ballistic missiles.

The SALT I agreement was a landmark in U.S.-Soviet relations. After more than twenty-five years of mutual aggression and refusal to compromise, a foundation had been laid for arms control. Plans were made for holding negotiations on a second agreement, known as SALT II.

LEAVING VIETNAM

The United States' new relationship with the Soviets and the Chinese helped the country extricate itself from Vietnam, as both communist powers put pressure on the North Vietnamese government to accept a peace agreement with the United States. While stepping up bombing attacks on North Vietnam, the United States opened secret negotiations with the senior North Vietnamese diplomat, Le Duc Tho. On January 27, 1973, a truce was finally signed, and shortly afterwards all U.S. troops were withdrawn from Vietnam. In 1975, North Vietnam seized control of South Vietnam.

▼ Nixon and Brezhnev (front right corner, left and right respectively) drink a toast following the signature of the SALT I agreement in Moscow.

THE FALL OF NIXON

By 1975, however, Richard Nixon was no longer U.S. president. Nixon's administration had been implicated in a break-in at the Democratic Party's offices in the Watergate complex, in Washington, D.C., during the 1972 presidential election campaign. Nixon attempted a cover-up, and the resulting scandal forced his resignation in 1974.

Vice President Gerald Ford replaced Nixon, but Henry Kissinger remained as secretary of state. The continuation of détente was a major foreign-policy goal for the new president. In November, 1974 Ford met with Brezhnev, and the two leaders established guidelines for the planned SALT II discussions. In August, 1975 Ford and Brezhnev also presided over an important conference held in Helsinki, Finland.

▲ Richard Nixon announcing his resignation, August 9, 1974. Tapes recorded in President Nixon's White House office proved his full involvement in the Watergate cover-up, and he chose to resign before the most incriminating tapes were released to the courts.

THE HELSINKI FINAL ACT

The Helsinki conference was attended by representatives of the United States, Soviet Union, and thirty-three European nations. Its main purpose was the final establishment of post-1945 boundaries in Europe. In addition, delegates hoped to adopt a range of other proposals that would foster both cooperation and security on a continent now divided between communist and democratic regimes.

The outcome of these discussions, the Helsinki Final Act, was signed on August 1, 1975. It confirmed existing borders in Europe, encouraged trade and other links between European nations, and sought the guarantee of human rights.

THE WAY AHEAD

Despite the upheaval of the Watergate scandal and Nixon's resignation, the future of détente appeared promising in 1976. Ford and Brezhnev were both committed to détente, if only for practical reasons, and friendly U.S.-Soviet relations seemed likely to continue. Unfortunately, those relations were about to take a turn for the worse. In January 1977, a new U.S. president took office, and the Cold War proved it had plenty of life left.

NIXON'S DÉTENTE

"An American President ... has a dual responsibility: He must resist Soviet expansionism. And he must be conscious of the profound risks of global confrontation. His policy must embrace both deterrence and coexistence, both containment and an effort to relax tensions ... That was what the Nixon Administration understood by détente."

HENRY KISSINGER, IN HIS BOOK *THE WHITE HOUSE YEARS*

CHAPTER TWO

The Collapse of Détente

The election of Democrat Jimmy Carter as U.S. president in 1976 marked the beginning of a difficult new period in the Cold War. In his inaugural address, Carter announced two firm foreign-policy goals: the promotion of human rights and the elimination of nuclear weapons. The new president, however, was less focused than his predecessors about his foreign-policy objectives. Over the next three years, the fragile détente built by Nixon and Ford slowly but surely collapsed.

▼ Following his election in November 1976, Jimmy Carter was inaugurated U.S. president on January 20, 1977. Here, Carter, his wife Rosalynn, and their daughter Amy walk past the cheering crowds after the ceremony.

Carter's uncertain approach to foreign policy in general and U.S.-Soviet relations in particular was made worse by the conflict between his two main advisers. Cyrus Vance, his secretary of state, wanted to revive the détente process and continue negotiations with the Soviets so that a SALT II treaty could quickly be reached. By contrast, Zbigniew Brzezinski, Carter's national security adviser, wanted the United States to focus on establishing supremacy over the Soviet Union, both

by increasing its stockpile of weapons and by strengthening the North Atlantic Treaty Organization (NATO), a defensive alliance of Western nations established in 1949.

Carter faced other difficulties as he built his foreign policy. First, the American public was weary of détente. Many Americans now saw détente not as a way to insure peace but as a sign of U.S. weakness. Second, Congress had severely limited presidential control of foreign policy. With the passage of the 1973 War Powers Act, a U.S. president had to ask Congress for approval before sending U.S. troops abroad. Congress also refused to lift trade restrictions on the Soviet Union, making it impossible to offer goods to the Soviets in exchange for compromise on political issues.

▲ As soon as he joined the Carter administration in 1977, Secretary of State Cyrus Vance committed himself to détente and arms reduction talks with the Soviet Union.

JIMMY CARTER (1924–)

Born in Georgia in 1924, Jimmy Carter joined the U.S. Navy in 1943. After his father died in the 1950s, Carter left military service to run the family's peanut business.

Carter served as both a state senator and the governor of Georgia. Voters knew him as a married man of great integrity, with a deep Christian faith. He emphasized these characteristics when he ran as the Democratic candidate for the presidency in 1976. Carter appealed to a nation recovering from the Watergate scandal, and he was elected.

While Carter brought many skills to the White House, including a high level of intelligence, he found it difficult to provide strong leadership. Although Carter helped to negotiate a major peace treaty between Israel and Egypt in 1979 and was an outspoken champion of human rights, his presidency is often remembered for its failures. These failures include his inability to formulate a clear Cold War policy, improve the ailing U.S. economy, or free U.S. hostages in Iran. Carter lost the 1980 presidential election to Republican Ronald Reagan. Since leaving office, he has worked for human rights worldwide.

RISING TENSIONS

Back in 1974, President Ford and Soviet premier Brezhnev had met in the Soviet port city of Vladivostok to prepare a framework for SALT II. The meeting had produced the Vladivostok Accord, which was an agreement that the United States and the Soviet Union would strive for equal numbers of nuclear missiles and missile launchers and at the same time work towards steadily reducing both. Because of the success of this accord, rapid progress on SALT II was expected.

In March 1977, when Cyrus Vance flew to Moscow to continue SALT II discussions, circumstances had changed dramatically. Not only was there a new president in the White House, but Soviet leader Brezhnev was losing his grip on power. Seriously ill after a possible stroke, he could not think or speak clearly. The Soviet regime had also been angered by a U.S. campaign for human rights in accordance with the Helsinki Final Act, and, perhaps most importantly, U.S. support for dissidents and Jews who wanted to emigrate from the Soviet Union.

The atmosphere at the negotiations soon went from bad to worse. Vance had brought a proposal for far greater arms reductions than had been agreed upon at Vladivostok. The Soviets regarded this as a clumsy effort to end their lead in intercontinental ballistic missiles (ICBMs), and in general they were upset that the Carter administration seemed so willing to set aside the Vladivostok Accord. Détente, they believed, was no longer a primary U.S. objective. Vance's proposal was rejected, and U.S.-Soviet relations were badly damaged.

CYRUS ROBERTS VANCE (1917–)

Cyrus Vance, who studied law at Yale University, first pursued a career in the U.S. Navy before practicing law. He then entered politics. Vance became secretary of state under the Carter administration in 1977, and for the next three years did his best to promote détente. He resigned in 1980, however, as a protest against the president's handling of the Iranian hostage crisis. In 1992, Vance returned to politics as a United Nations negotiator at the peace talks in Bosnia-Herzegovina, formerly the Yugoslav republic, which had been ravaged by civil war. Vance retired in 1993 as a result of ill health.

MORE MISSILES

As the political situation deteriorated, both sides began improving their weapons systems. In 1977, the Soviet Union replaced many old missiles in Eastern Europe with more accurate

SS-20s, which were intermediate-range missiles designed to hit targets in Western Europe rather than in the United States. This development alarmed Western European governments, who were also angry that the United States had decided to exclude such weapons from consideration in SALT II.

The United States, meanwhile, increased defense spending and urged its European allies in NATO to do likewise. They responded with the promise of a yearly three percent increase. In mid-1977, the United States began to develop a new type of intermediate-range cruise missile, as well as a new military aircraft, the Stealth bomber. Despite these aggressive moves, however, Carter still supported the SALT talks. This seemingly contradictory approach was largely the result of the opposing foreign-policy advice that the president often received from Brzezinski and Vance.

Intermediate-range cruise missiles had to be stationed in Europe if they were to reach the Soviet Union, and so did the new U.S. Pershing II ballistic missiles. During 1978, the United States worked hard persuading the British, West Germans, Italians, Belgians, and Dutch to accept the installation of U.S. weapons on their soil.

▼ The Soviet Union's intermediate-range SS-20 missiles posed a direct threat to the European members of NATO. The missiles were also intended to warn the United States against increasing its nuclear installations in Europe.

11

Leonid Brezhnev (left) and Jimmy Carter (right) signed the SALT II treaty in Vienna, Austria, on June 18, 1979.

MAIN TERMS OF SALT II

- Neither nation to possess more than 2,400 missiles, and all missiles and launchers beyond that number allowed to be destroyed

- Both nations to reduce missile numbers to 2,250 by 1981

- Neither nation to have more than 1,200 ICBMs (intercontinental ballistic missiles) and SLBMs (submarine-launched ballistic missiles)

- Each nation's MIRVs (multiple independently targeted reentry vehicles), which possess multiple warheads aimed at different targets, to have no more than ten warheads each

- Neither nation permitted to make on-site inspections of the other nation's missiles or missile-destruction programs

SALT II AND AFTER

Despite the setbacks in U.S.-Soviet relations since the original 1972 SALT I agreement and the 1974 Vladivostok Accord, negotiations for SALT II had still continued. Finally, on June 18, 1979, President Carter and Soviet premier Brezhnev met in Vienna, Austria, where they signed the SALT II treaty. The treaty's main provisions restricted both nations to no more than 2,400 missiles each and required them to reduce that number to 2,250 by 1981. Plans were also made for the development of a SALT III treaty.

Carter was not able to enjoy his SALT II victory for long. Back home, he faced serious opposition from the U.S. Senate, which had to ratify the SALT II agreement before it could take effect. Many members of the Senate were in no mood to approve what they saw as concessions to the Soviet Union, and the American public seemed to feel the same way. Many Americans now agreed with such politicians as Ronald Reagan, who had unsuccessfully sought the Republican nomination for president in 1976 and who preached hard-line resistance to the Soviet Union.

RETURN OF THE ARMS RACE

National Security Adviser Zbigniew Brzezinski was pleased at this new turn of events, because he knew that Carter would now have to take a firmer stand against the Soviets to regain political support. Brzezinski urged Carter to allow the development of the MX missile, which was meant to replace the existing Minuteman ICBM, and the president had little choice but to agree. The United States was already developing the Trident submarine, which could carry ICBMs with nuclear warheads. In the United States, the arms race was now back.

Developments in Europe added to growing U.S.-Soviet tensions. In January 1979, West German chancellor Helmut Schmidt and British prime minister James Callaghan had agreed to allow the installation of U.S. cruise and Pershing II ballistic missile sites in their countries. The two leaders had bowed to U.S. pressure, but they had also seen the necessity of deterring Soviet aggression against European targets. Despite some fierce opposition from the German and British people, the leaders held to their decisions. At a meeting in Brussels on December 12, 1979, all NATO nations approved the deployment of new U.S. weapons in Western Europe.

ZBIGNIEW BRZEZINSKI (1928–)

Zbigniew Brzezinski was born in Poland, a country that for much of its history suffered greatly at the hands of Russians. He was educated at McGill University in Canada and Harvard University but never forgot his Polish roots. After becoming President Carter's national security adviser, Brzezinski declared himself "the first Pole in three hundred years in a position to really stick it to the Russians." Not surprisingly, he took a strong anti-détente stance throughout Carter's term in office. When Ronald Reagan began his first term as U.S. president in January, 1981, Brzezinski left government. He then became professor of political science at Columbia University in New York City.

◀ Many Europeans protested the installation of U.S. missiles on their continent. One organized group that opposed U.S. missiles in Europe was the Danish group Women for Peace, which supported a "peace camp" at the U.S. air base in Greenham Common, Britain. At left, a group member collects signatures against the use of land mines.

Soviet helicopters at the airport in Kabul, the capital of Afghanistan, in January 1980. In 1985, at the height of the conflict in Afghanistan, over 120,000 Red Army troops were stationed in the country.

INVASION OF AFGHANISTAN

The final blow to détente came in December 1979, when the Soviet Union invaded Afghanistan, a mountainous, arid country on its southern border. During the 1970s, Afghanistan became strongly pro-Soviet and introduced many communist policies. Its government, however, faced violent opposition from fundamentalist Islamic rebels, known as *mujaheddin*. While the Soviets wanted to help the government resist this threat, they were reluctant to send in troops.

The situation changed in 1979, when a new Afghan ruler, Hafizullah Amin, seized power. Previously a committed communist, Amin now began to seek Western support. The Soviets were not about to let the government of Afghanistan ally itself with the United States, and on December 25, 1979, Soviet Red Army troops invaded the country. Within five days, Amin was dead and a Soviet-backed leader, Babrak Karmal, had taken his place.

U.S. RESPONSE

The United States was furious with the Soviet intervention in Afghanistan. U.S. leaders feared that the invasion was the first stage of a Soviet plan to seize control of neighboring Iran and the oil-rich Persian Gulf region. President Carter reacted quickly. He withdrew SALT II from the ratification process, increased defense spending, banned grain and high-technology sales to the Soviet Union, and ordered a U.S. boycott of the 1980 Moscow Olympics.

The Soviets had neither wanted nor predicted such an angry response. They had estimated that the intervention in Afghanistan would last only a few weeks, would end once a new leader had been imposed, and would cause little stir in the West. Instead they found themselves locked in a lengthy struggle that did great harm to the process of détente.

President Carter summed up the U.S. view of the Afghanistan invasion on January 23, 1980, in his annual State of the Union speech. In the speech, Carter called the Soviet intervention "the most serious threat to peace since the Second World War." Carter also warned the Soviets that advances into the Persian Gulf would be resisted by any means necessary, a statement that became known as the Carter Doctrine. For the United States, détente was now over and a new phase of the Cold War was about to begin.

THE CARTER DOCTRINE

"… the region now threatened by Soviet troops in Afghanistan is of great strategic importance: it contains more than two-thirds of the world's exportable oil. The Soviet effort to dominate Afghanistan has brought Soviet military forces to within 300 miles of the Indian Ocean and close to the Straits of Hormuz — a waterway through which much of the free world's oil must flow. The Soviet Union is attempting to consolidate a strategic position that poses a grave threat to the free movement of Middle East oil … let our position be absolutely clear. Any attempt by any outside force to gain control of the Persian Gulf will be regarded as an assault on the vital interests of the United States. And such an assault will be repelled by any means necessary, including military force."

PRESIDENT CARTER, IN HIS STATE OF THE UNION SPEECH, JANUARY 23, 1980 (THE FINAL TWO SENTENCES CONSTITUTE THE CARTER DOCTRINE.)

◄ The opening ceremony of the 1980 Moscow Olympics. The United States, West Germany, and several other nations boycotted the games in protest against the Soviet invasion of Afghanistan. The Soviets retaliated by boycotting the 1984 Los Angeles Olympics.

CHAPTER THREE

Cold War II

U.S. presidents Nixon, Ford, and Carter all opposed the communist ideology of the Soviet Union. Yet as political realists, they were also prepared to make concessions to the Soviets to avoid crippling the U.S. economy and plunging the world into war. Carter's successor, however, the Republican president Ronald Reagan, adopted a different strategy in dealing with the Soviets. For him, the conflict between the democratic United States and the communist Soviet Union was a struggle between good and evil, and he was ready to launch another cold war to ensure that good prevailed.

DÉTENTE ENDS

▼ President Ronald Reagan during inaugural celebrations in January 1981. Standing beside Reagan is his wife, Nancy, who devotedly supported the president throughout his eight years in office.

After Reagan defeated Carter in the 1980 presidential election and took office in January 1981, he struggled to comprehend the finer points of U.S. foreign affairs. Reagan was absolutely certain, however, about his broad policy of containing Soviet influence. The United States would build up its military strength and reassert its status as the world's leading superpower. Détente, already sidelined by the Soviet invasion of Afghanistan, would now be completely abandoned.

PREPARING FOR WAR

With the help of his defense secretary, Caspar Weinberger, Reagan initiated a massive arms buildup. His plan called for increasing the defense budget from $171 billion in 1981 to $367.5 billion in 1986. A new type of bomber, the B-1, was to be introduced, and the navy was to gain 144 ships, for a total of 600. The number of conventional (nonnuclear) weapons available to U.S. military forces would also be increased.

SOVIET RESPONSE

The Soviets, who in 1981 were still under the leadership of the ailing Brezhnev, eyed these developments warily. Yet the dismal condition of the Soviet economy — by the 1980s, it was growing by three percent a year, compared with ten percent in the 1950s — made expansion of the Soviet defense budget a difficult option. In 1981, Brezhnev himself proclaimed to Soviet colleagues, "We do not support the arms race, we oppose it. We could find a totally different use for the funds it swallows up."

A renewed military buildup had other drawbacks. The Soviet Union desperately needed Western technology and was also dependent on the West's grain imports to feed its people. To guarantee the continuing supply of these goods, many in the Soviet leadership wanted to restore, not destroy, détente. There was also a growing view among the Soviets that it would be impossible to "win" a nuclear war, and that such wars were best avoided altogether. Since a revived Soviet arms program would increase tensions and make conflict more likely, it was best avoided, too.

RONALD WILSON REAGAN (1911–)

Ronald Reagan was born in Tampico, Illinois. In 1937, after he had worked as a sports announcer on a radio station, he moved to Hollywood, where he became an actor and appeared in over fifty films. During his years in Hollywood, Reagan turned against the Democratic politics he had once supported, believing they encouraged too much invasion of privacy by the government. He also gave evidence to the House Committee on Un-American Activities, which had been created to investigate suspected communist activity. In 1962, Reagan joined the Republican Party.

From 1967 to 1975, Reagan served as the governor of California, where his sharp political skills and easy charm won him many admirers. After failing to win the Republican presidential nomination in 1968 and 1976, he won the nomination in 1980. He was elected president in 1980 and again in 1984.

Reagan focused his domestic policy on cutting taxes and reducing welfare. At the same time, he also pursued an aggressive anticommunist foreign policy. His negotiations with Soviet leader Mikhail Gorbachev played a major role in ending the Cold War. Reagan was succeeded by his vice president, George Bush, in 1989.

PROBLEMS IN POLAND

Since World War II, the governments of Eastern Europe had mostly been communist regimes that were under firm Soviet control. In the 1980s, however, the Soviet Union began to lose its influence in Eastern Europe. The trouble began in Poland, where popular resistance to the communist government started to rise after the 1979 visit of Polish-born Pope John Paul II.

SHORTAGES AND STRIKES

Following President Carter's suspension of détente, the United States cut back severely on its exports to the Soviets and their Eastern European satellite countries. Poland, which had long suffered from shortages of food and consumer goods, was hit especially hard. When the Polish government, led by Edward Gierek, made matters worse by doubling meat prices in July 1980, protest strikes spread across the country. A poor harvest later that year only fueled tensions.

▼ Solidarity leader Lech Walesa (right) with Poland's deputy prime minister Mieczyslaw Jagielski in August 1980. The Polish government's recognition of Solidarity and acceptance of its early demands were not enough to prevent further unrest in Poland.

BIRTH OF SOLIDARITY

A major center of Polish unrest was the Lenin shipyard, in the port city of Gdansk on the Baltic coast. When a strike began at the shipyard in mid-August, the government attempted to get people back to work by beginning negotiations over pay, as it had elsewhere. The desire for change, however, could not be kept down. That month, a charismatic, unemployed electrician named Lech Walesa led thousands of Gdansk workers to form a trade union. It was called *Solidarnosc*, which is Polish for "solidarity."

Although Soviet leaders were infuriated when the Polish government recognized the new union, they decided not to send in troops immediately. Instead they ordered the government to do everything in its power to defeat the Solidarity movement. Gierek was replaced by a more aggressive leader, Stanislaw Kania. The United States, meanwhile, was secretly supporting Walesa and his followers.

A GROWING MOVEMENT

The Soviet Union's nonmilitary approach did not work. Soon Solidarity had some ten million members and their demands grew daily. Economic improvements, such as better pay, were no longer enough. Now Solidarity members were determined to achieve political change too.

These developments led to mounting alarm in Moscow. Soviet leaders knew they had to act decisively and began drawing up plans for military intervention. Yet they also understood that Solidarity was supported by both Western democracies and the Roman Catholic Church. Repression of Solidarity by force would probably provoke international condemnation and an escalation of the Cold War.

▲ A stern-faced General Wojciech Jaruzelski declares martial law in 1981.

MARTIAL LAW

The Polish government ultimately solved its own problems. On February 9, 1981, General Wojciech Jaruzelski, Poland's former defense minister, took over as the country's leader. The Soviets were content to work through Jaruzelski, who was a hard-line communist, and encouraged him to neutralize Solidarity by whatever means necessary.

Solidarity, however, continued to gain support, and by late 1981 Poland was descending into chaos as strikes and anti-communist protests erupted across the country. Finally, on December 13, 1981, Jaruzelski declared martial law.

The Polish government now began to move fast. Solidarity was banned, Lech Walesa was arrested, and troops were sent into the streets to restore order. Poland was back under the Soviets' control. Yet the Polish people now knew their own power, and soon they and many other Eastern Europeans began to fight back against communist regimes.

POLAND'S UPRISING

"… the working men and women of Poland have set an example for all those who cherish freedom and dignity."

PRESIDENT JIMMY CARTER, SEPTEMBER 1980

"Solidarity has been transformed into an organized political force, which is able to paralyze the activity of the party and state organs and take *de facto* power into its own hands. If [Solidarity] has not yet done that, then it is primarily because of its fear that Soviet troops would be introduced and because of its hopes that it can achieve its aims without bloodshed and by means of a creeping counterrevolution."

THE SOVIET POLITBURO, APRIL 1981

SALT II AND START

Although Congress never ratified the SALT II treaty, in 1982 President Reagan promised the Soviet Union that if it did not break the terms of the treaty, neither would the United States. At the request of Congress, Reagan also proposed a new round of SALT negotiations, to be renamed START (Strategic Arms Reduction Talks). START negotiation began in June 1982, in Geneva, Switzerland. Prospects for START were not good, however, since the United States was unwilling to cut back any of its main long-range systems, such as the MX ICBM.

"ZERO OPTION"

While START negotiations were being held, the United States and the Soviet Union also held Intermediate-Range Nuclear Forces (INF) talks. The talks dealt with shorter-range nuclear missiles, which the Soviets had targeted at Western Europe

▼ At Leonid Brezhnev's funeral in November 1982, leading members of the Soviet Communist Party carry his open casket. The man at the front wearing glasses is Brezhnev's successor, Yuri Andropov.

and the United States wanted to install in Europe to hit targets in the Soviet Union. These weapons included the U.S. cruise and Pershing II missiles, which had not yet been deployed, and the Soviet SS-4, SS-5, and SS-20 missiles.

Unfortunately, no real progress was made on the INF talks. Since so many Europeans did not want the new U.S. missiles on their soil, the United States proposed a "zero option." It offered to stop the deployment of its new cruise and Pershing II missiles if the Soviet Union removed the SS-4, SS-5, and SS-20 missiles pointed at Western Europe. The Soviets, however, were not prepared to give up so much, and the talks dragged on into 1983.

YURI ANDROPOV

In November 1982, Leonid Brezhnev died and was quickly replaced as Soviet leader by Yuri Andropov. Like Brezhnev before him, Andropov was old and in poor health, and he had taken charge of a country with a crumbling economy but massive military commitments.

Andropov's main goal was improving the Soviet Union's economy in order to strengthen his country's international standing. He set out to renew détente by making several proposals, including an offer to reduce the number of SS-20 missiles targeting Europe. Andropov also hoped that European peace protesters would persuade the United States not to deploy its new weapons.

LEONID ILYICH BREZHNEV (1906–1982)

Originally from the Ukraine, in the southwestern region of the Soviet Union, Brezhnev joined the Communist Party as a young man and rose gradually through the party ranks. In 1952, his skills were noticed by Soviet leader Joseph Stalin, and he was then quickly brought into the Politburo, the Soviet government's main policy-making body. Upon Stalin's death in 1953, Brezhnev lost his post in Moscow, but he was restored to a position of power by new Soviet leader Nikita Khrushchev, whom Brezhnev had known in the Ukraine. After Khrushchev was ousted in 1964, Brezhnev took over as Communist Party general secretary.

A dull, uninspiring man, Brezhnev nevertheless introduced a dynamic foreign policy based on increasing Soviet military spending and influence abroad. In 1968, when the Soviet troops invaded Czechoslovakia to maintain communist rule, Brezhnev formulated the Brezhnev Doctrine, which held that the Soviet Union had the right to enforce Soviet-backed communism in the countries under its control.

In 1976 Brezhnev became seriously ill, having most likely suffered a stroke. The rest of the Soviet leadership hid his condition, however, and, ruling on his behalf, made the decision to invade Afghanistan in 1979. After struggling with ill health for six years, Brezhnev died in 1982 at the age of seventy-five.

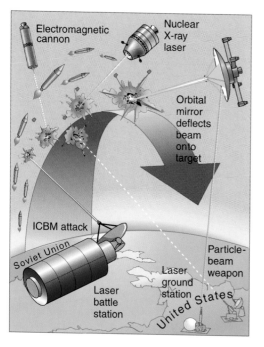

Electromagnetic cannon

Nuclear X-ray laser

Orbital mirror deflects beam onto target

ICBM attack

Soviet Union

Laser battle station

Laser ground station

Particle-beam weapon

United States

This diagram of the SDI system shows how particle beams, nuclear X-ray lasers, and electromagnetic cannon would work together to stop incoming Soviet missiles.

STAR WARS

In the spring of 1983, as Yuri Andropov was attempting to put his country's relationship with the United States on a more friendly footing, President Reagan denounced the Soviet Union as an "evil empire." Reagan then proposed the Strategic Defense Initiative (SDI). The program, which involved a space-based weapons system that Reagan claimed would protect the United States from missile attack, was soon dubbed "Star Wars."

A PERFECT PLAN?

Even on paper, SDI was a complex, ambitious plan. Utilizing such futuristic weapons as lasers, particle beams, and electromagnetic cannon, SDI was supposed to provide the United States with an impenetrable shield that would intercept all incoming missiles. The plan showed promise, but it also had flaws. Much of the SDI technology was still in the early stages of development, and no one was exactly sure how much the system would cost or even if it would work at all. Yet despite its shortcomings, SDI had a dramatic impact on world relations.

First, SDI threatened to upset the Cold War's balance of power. For almost forty years, the United States and the Soviet Union had been kept in check by the knowledge that one side's nuclear attack would unleash a devastating retaliation from the other side. This nuclear deterrence would disappear if the United States was no longer vulnerable, and when the Soviets learned of SDI, they vowed to develop missiles capable of penetrating the SDI shield.

Second, SDI strained relations between the United States and its democratic allies in Western Europe. An SDI shield would offer them no protection and might actually make them more likely to be hit by Soviet missiles. Reagan, however, was determined to go ahead with SDI. Despite some resistance, he soon secured $14.68 billion in SDI funding from Congress.

FLIGHT KAL 007

In 1983, as the relationship between the United States and the Soviet Union went from bad to worse, an incident occurred that helped to fuel the deteriorating situation. On August 31, 1983, a Korean Airlines passenger jet traveling from Alaska to Seoul left its flight path and entered Soviet airspace. Apparently believing the commercial jet was a spy plane, the Soviets shot it down, killing all 269 people on board.

The tragedy of flight KAL 007 provoked outrage from the United States and other countries, and the Soviets' clumsy and unconvincing efforts to defend themselves did not help matters. While the question of why KAL 007 strayed so far from its flight path remains a mystery, at the time the United States saw the episode as proof of the Soviets' barbaric ways.

TALKS END

The year 1983 drew to a close with another setback. In November, U.S. Pershing II ballistic missiles and ground-launched cruise missiles were deployed in Britain and West Germany. The Soviets considered this to be a sign that the United States was not committed to the START and INF talks being held in Geneva, and the Soviet negotiators walked out.

MILITARY POWER: UNITED STATES vs. SOVIET UNION, 1983–1984

	U.S.	Soviet
Intercontinental ballistic missiles	1,045	1,398
Submarine-launched ballistic missiles	568	980
Long-range strategic bombers	272	143
Total delivery vehicles (ICBMs, SLBMs, bombers)	1,885	2,521
Nuclear warheads (ICBMs and SLBMs)	7,297	8,343
Destructive power (in millions of tons of TNT)	2,202	5,111
Antiballistic missile launchers (ABM)	0	32
Aircraft carriers	14	5
Armed forces personnel	2,136,400	5,050,000

SIGNS OF HOPE

In 1984, President Reagan began to soften the tone of his remarks about the Soviet Union, in part to avoid alienating moderate voters during an election year. Instead, Reagan began speaking openly about the need for more arms control.

In the Soviet Union, Yuri Andropov's brief term of office ended with his death on February 9, 1984. He was replaced by Konstantin Chernenko, another aging politician in bad health. Chernenko was so ill with emphysema that his spell in power proved even shorter than Andropov's. The Soviets' paralyzing distrust of the United States, meanwhile, made real progress in U.S.-Soviet relations difficult.

▼ President Reagan's secretary of state, George Shultz (left), and Soviet foreign minister Andrei Gromyko meet in Geneva in January 1985. While Shultz smiles for the cameras, Gromyko is not so enthusiastic.

REVIVING THE ARMS TALKS

In January 1984, as part of his new approach to the Soviet Union, Reagan sent his secretary of state, George Shultz, to meet Soviet foreign minister Andrei Gromyko. Discussions between the two officials were lengthy and constructive. At a United Nations meeting in November, Reagan talked with Gromyko himself and came away impressed. Reagan was reelected soon after the meeting, and he arranged for Shultz and Gromyko to meet again in January 1985, with the hope that they could revive the arms control talks that had ended so disastrously in late 1983.

A LEADER IN WAITING?

While Chernenko lived out his last months as Soviet leader, younger men in the Soviet leadership were preparing to introduce new ways of approaching the Cold War's old problems. Among these men was Mikhail Gorbachev, already an important Politburo member. In December 1984, he met in London with British prime minister Margaret Thatcher. While Thatcher was a loyal supporter of Reagan and his anticommunist stance, she was still impressed by this dynamic man, who seemed like a Soviet leader in waiting.

REAGAN IN CHINA

Relations between the United States and communist China, meanwhile, were changing for the better. Since President Nixon's 1972 visit to China, U.S. relations with the country had not gone beyond exchanging ambassadors in 1979. The lukewarm relations were partly due to U.S. arms sales to Taiwan, where Chinese anticommunists still plotted their return to power on the mainland. By the mid-1980s, however, even Reagan had accepted that the communists had control of China. While the United States no longer needed China as an ally in its struggle against the Soviets, Reagan visited the country in April 1984.

WINNING FRIENDS

"I like Mr. Gorbachev. We can do business together."

British prime minister Margaret Thatcher, December 1984

CHAPTER FOUR

War Around The World

One enduring aspect of the Cold War was the fact that the United States and the Soviet Union rarely engaged each other directly. Instead, the clash of ideologies between the two superpowers turned into a global struggle where each side intervened in any conflict that needed its support. The main battlegrounds of the Cold War had been Eastern Europe, Korea, Cuba, and Vietnam. Yet in the 1970s and 1980s, the Cold War touched many other parts of the world too.

EL SALVADOR

The Reagan administration did not confine its intervention in Central America to Nicaragua. In 1979, the Farabundo Marti National Liberation Front (FMLN), a left-wing guerrilla group, challenged El Salvador's ruling right-wing party. It failed to win power, however, and a civilian-military junta (regime) seized control. Under its rule, human rights abuses became common. In 1980 Oscar Romero, archbishop of the country's capital, San Salvador, was assassinated; soon after, three American nuns were also killed. President Carter then suspended U.S. aid, but he restored it in early 1981, when the FMLN launched an attack on the junta.

During Reagan's first term in office, aid to the junta was increased from $36 million in 1981 to $197 million in 1984. Reagan insisted that José Napoleon Duarte, El Salvador's president for much of the 1980s, was a moderate leader who deserved U.S. support against the left-wing FMLN. Under Duarte's rule, however, the junta sent out military "death squads" that killed about 40,000 civilians.

TROUBLE IN NICARAGUA

The United States had always been anxious to stop communism from taking hold in Central America, a region it considered to be its own backyard. To fight the spread of communism, the United States had even been willing to support ruthless right-wing dictators who showed little regard for human rights.

General Anastasio Somoza was just such a dictator. Somoza's wealthy family had ruled Nicaragua since 1936, and the general's regime was often brutally oppressive. In 1979, left-wing Sandinista rebels overthrew General Somoza and established a government led by Daniel Ortega Saavedra.

President Carter responded cautiously. He did not care for the new government but still sent financial aid, which seemed wiser than forcing the Sandinistas to turn to the Soviets or communist Cuba. Yet the Cubans became involved anyway. Carter reduced the aid before leaving office, and Reagan, who opposed the Sandinista regime, stopped the aid entirely in 1981. The Cubans now played a larger role, providing doctors and other experts to the Sandinistas.

SUPPORTING THE CONTRAS

The Reagan administration was not alone in its dislike of the Sandinistas. Many middle-class Nicaraguans had lost power and property under Sandinista rule, and they backed an armed resistance group known as the Contras. In 1981, civil war erupted as the Contras sought to overthrow Ortega and the Sandinista government. That same year, the Reagan administration began supporting the Contras with money, arms, and military training.

In 1983, however, Reagan's request for more money to continue funding the Contras was turned down by Congress. A year later, Congress passed the Boland Amendment, which clearly stated that no further government money was to be spent in Central America.

THE IRAN-CONTRA AFFAIR

Because Reagan was not prepared to end U.S. support of the Contras, a complex and illegal funding arrangement was ultimately created. In the early 1980s, the United States began to supply Iran with arms in return for hostages. Then a Marine officer, Lieutenant Colonel Oliver North, conceived of the idea of using profits from the Iranian arms sales to fund the Contras. It is unclear whether Reagan knew what North was doing. When the scheme was discovered in November 1986, however, the public's faith in Reagan was severely shaken.

GRENADA

The United States' third intervention in Latin America took place on the small Caribbean island of Grenada. Since 1979, the island had been ruled by a leftist government with Cuban ties. When hard-line leftists overthrew that government in 1983, Reagan sent 1,900 U.S. troops to the island and a pro-U.S. government was installed. Reagan claimed that U.S. intervention had kept Grenada from becoming a Soviet-Cuban colony.

▼ Oliver North, the man who implemented the illegal Contras funding scheme, testifying before a 1987 Congressional hearing. North argued that his conduct was a justifiable way of stopping the spread of communism.

THE COLD WAR IN AFRICA

Although Africa had been a patchwork of European colonies in the early part of the twentieth century, by the 1950s one colony after another began struggling for independence. In many cases, these emerging countries were deeply divided by opposing factions who were prepared to use violence to gain control. One such country was Angola, where a complex situation was further complicated by the Cold War.

UNREST IN ANGOLA

Located in southwest Africa, Angola had been a Portuguese colony since the fifteenth century, but in the 1950s a nationalist movement for independence began. By 1961, the movement had turned into a guerrilla war against the Portuguese. Three different guerrilla groups, each with different political views and loyalties to different tribes, led the war. The communist Movement for the Liberation of Angola (MPLA) consisted of mixed tribes. The anticommunist National Front for the Liberation of Angola (FNLA) was supported by the Bakongo tribe. Most members of the National Union for the Total Independence of Angola (UNITA) belonged to the Ovimbundu tribe, but their political allegiance was not clear-cut.

▼ In this 1976 scene from the Angolan civil war, U.S.-backed UNITA soldiers inspect a railway bridge that has been destroyed by Soviet-backed MPLA forces.

SUPERPOWER INVOLVEMENT

The United States and the Soviet Union were eager to gain influence in Angola, both for political reasons and to acquire an interest in the country's oil, gas, and diamond reserves. Each superpower backed the guerrilla force that most closely shared its ideology, with the Soviets supporting the MPLA and the United States supporting the FNLA. Other nations also became involved. The Cubans, for example, provided the MPLA with military training, while the Chinese backed the FNLA in an effort to stop the influence of their Soviet rivals in the region.

INDEPENDENCE AND ITS AFTERMATH

In April 1974, the dictator of Portugal, Antonio Salazar, was overthrown, and in January 1975 Portugal's new government announced that Angola would be granted independence in November. At first, the guerrilla groups appeared willing to work together. When the superpowers increased military and financial aid to the groups, however, cooperation evaporated. Ironically, independence had only helped fuel more unrest.

Other factors contributed to the rising violence. In mid-1975, the United States began to fund the UNITA as well as the FNLA, and anticommunist South Africa also sent troops to fight alongside UNITA forces. The Cubans and the Soviets responded with massive increases for the MPLA.

THE PEOPLE'S REPUBLIC OF ANGOLA

The Ford administration, denied more funds by Congress, could do nothing more for the FNLA and UNITA, and South Africa's withdrawal of troops ensured MPLA victory. In 1976, the MPLA established the People's Republic of Angola, based in Luanda, and signed a friendship treaty with the Soviets. In Huambo, meanwhile, the FNLA and UNITA established the People's Democratic Republic of Angola, which won little international recognition. The United States had lost this Cold War battle. When fighting in Angola began again, however, it secretly supported the anti-MPLA rebels.

▼ In 1977, troops from Somalia in northeast Africa invaded neighboring Ethiopia's Ogaden desert, but with Soviet help the Ethiopians forced them out the following year. This photograph shows young Somali troops in a training camp located in captured Ethiopian territory.

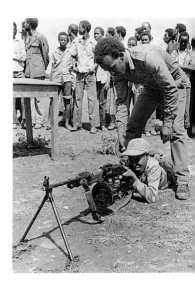

HOSTAGES IN IRAN

An important source of oil production for the West and a longtime U.S. ally, Iran underwent drastic change in the 1970s. Iran's ruler, Shah Mohammed Reza Pahlavi, became increasingly unpopular with the Iranian people. His attempts to "Westernize" Iranian society angered many Iranians, particularly fundamentalist Muslims who wanted to preserve traditional values.

In 1978, rioting finally broke out, and in January 1979 the shah fled Iran. Soon after, Ayatollah Ruholla Khomeini, a Muslim cleric who had been living in exile, returned to Iran and established an Islamic government that was deeply hostile to the United States. In October 1979 the shah entered the United States for medical treatment, and on November 4, 1979, Iranian students protested by taking over the U.S. embassy in the capital city of Teheran and holding fifty-eight Americans hostage.

President Carter did not handle the crisis well. First, he made several unsuccessful attempts to negotiate the hostages' release. Then, wrongly fearing that the Soviets were about to intervene, he warned them that he would invoke the Carter Doctrine. Finally, in April 1980, Carter authorized a helicopter rescue mission to Teheran. The mission was a humiliating and tragic failure, and was partly responsible for his defeat in the 1980 presidential election. The hostages were finally released in January 1981, just as Ronald Reagan took office.

COLD WAR IN THE MIDDLE EAST

From the earliest days of the Cold War, the United States had been determined to prevent Soviet influence in the Middle East, for a simple reason: more than sixty percent of the West's oil supplies came from the region. The Soviet Union, however, was not about to leave the Middle East alone.

In the 1960s and 1970s this rivalry fueled conflict in a volatile region. Since the establishment of the Jewish state of Israel in 1948, the country had been the target of intense and unending hostility from its Arab neighbors.

TAKING SIDES

During the 1960s, the Soviets supplied several Arab states with weapons and supported them in disputes with Israel. The United States, on the other hand, usually allied itself with the Israeli cause. This division of interests became more severe after the Six-Day War of 1967, during which the Israelis dramatically defeated Egypt, Jordan, and Syria. After the war, the Soviets established bases in Egypt and also supplied the country with military equipment.

Egypt's relationship with the Soviet Union changed in 1972, when Egyptian president Anwar Sadat claimed that the Soviets were more interested in the SALT I treaty with the United States than in helping Egypt recover territory lost in the Six-Day War. In protest, Sadat expelled all Soviet military experts from his country. Yet in October 1973, when Egypt and Syria launched

a surprise attack on Israel during the Jewish religious holiday of Yom Kippur, the Soviets nonetheless sided with the Arabs, while the United States sided with the Israelis. Tensions ran high during the conflict — at one point the United States was on nuclear alert — but a cease-fire was finally established.

▲ Egyptian president Anwar Sadat (left), U.S. president Jimmy Carter (center), and Israeli prime minister Menachem Begin (right) clasp hands in friendship after their Camp David meetings in September 1978.

CAMP DAVID

In 1973, U.S. secretary of state Henry Kissinger began playing a central role in promoting Middle East peace. Flying regularly between Egypt, Syria, and Israel, he slowly drew the opposing sides closer together. The Soviets were excluded from all of these talks.

Prospects for peace increased in 1977, when Sadat visited Israel. The following year, Sadat and Israeli prime minister Menachem Begin joined President Carter at his Camp David retreat. This meeting led to the Camp David Accords, which was a framework for future negotiations. A peace treaty between Egypt and Israel was finally signed in 1979. Under its terms the Sinai Peninsula, seized by Israel during the Six-Day War, was returned.

The 1979 treaty was important but limited. In particular, it failed to address the West Bank, another territory won by the Israelis in 1967 that was home to thousands of Palestinians. Many Arab states refused to accept the treaty, as did the Soviets. In the Middle East, the Cold War divide was just as broad and as dangerous as it had ever been.

LEBANON

Lebanon, to the north of Israel, was another country where the United States and the Soviet Union clashed. Lebanon suffered from many internal divisions, the most notable being between Christians and Muslims, who began a civil war in 1975. The country was also home to thousands of Palestinians who had fled their homeland after the foundation of Israel. Many of these Palestinian refugees belonged to the Palestine Liberation Organization (PLO), which launched regular rocket attacks on the Israelis from Lebanon.

In 1982, the Israelis, using U.S. arms, invaded Lebanon to punish the PLO. The Syrians defended the Palestinians, using Soviet weapons. U.S. Marines were then sent to Lebanon as part of a UN peace-keeping force, and they soon became involved in the civil war, provoking Muslim hostility. Congress asked Reagan to pull the troops out, but he refused, claiming they were protecting Lebanon from Soviet influence. In 1983, a Muslim terrorist drove a truck packed with explosives into the U.S. barracks in Lebanon, killing 239 men. Reagan then had the troops withdrawn from the country.

CHAPTER FIVE

New Political Thinking

Soviet leader Konstantin Chernenko died on March 10, 1985, after little more than a year in office. The next day, Mikhail Gorbachev took his place as general secretary of the Soviet Communist Party. Gorbachev's *novoye myshlenniye*, which is Russian for "new political thinking," would transform both his own country and its relations with the West in just a few eventful years.

THE SOVIET ECONOMY

Even before coming to power, Gorbachev had taken a long, hard look at the stumbling Soviet economy. Military spending swallowed about half of the Soviet Union's gross national product. Aid to Cuba, Afghanistan, and other communist allies also drained resources, costing up to $40 billion per year. Tight governmental control of industry, meanwhile, had stifled initiative, leading to low output. Every citizen felt the effects of the Soviet mismanagement of the economy. Wages and living standards were low, and housing was poor.

▼ During the Soviet era, when food shortages were common across the Soviet Union, people often waited in long lines for such basic goods as bread.

TIME FOR REFORM

Gorbachev understood that the only way to avoid economic disaster was to introduce radical reforms. These reforms fell into two basic categories. The first was *perestroika*, or restructuring of the economy. The second was *glasnost*, or increased political openness. Since Gorbachev knew it would be impossible to restructure the economy without cutting military spending, he set out to reestablish arms reduction negotiations with the United States.

A NEW START

Soviet foreign minister Andrei Gromyko and U.S. secretary of state George Shultz had already met, in January 1985. At talks in Geneva, the two men agreed to revive the START and INF negotiations and also begin discussions about defense systems such as SDI. After a few months it was also agreed that Gorbachev and Reagan should hold a summit conference in November 1985.

During the summer and autumn of 1985, Gorbachev prepared for this summit. In July, he replaced dour Foreign Minister Gromyko with the more charismatic Eduard Shevardnadze, a man who shared his total commitment to change. Along with Shevardnadze, Gorbachev then formulated a new approach to Soviet relations with the Western democracies.

▲ Soviet foreign minister Eduard Shevardnadze (left) meets his Danish counterpart Uffe Ellemann Jensen in September 1988.

This approach was based on three core beliefs. The first belief was that the superpower rivalry was both damaging and pointless. The arms race could never be won and would instead continue endlessly as first one power and then the other edged ahead. The second was that superpower backing of military conflicts in developing countries had achieved little at great cost. Joint humanitarian aid would be a far-better option. The third belief, which followed from the first two, was that lasting peace and security could only be achieved through politics.

Gorbachev also intended for the Soviet government to show greater concern for freedom of speech and other human rights. He believed this change would ease relations with the West, which had long criticized the Soviet Union's harsh repression of dissent.

MAKING PROGRESS

"We [the Soviet leadership] understand that in today's world of mutual interdependence, progress is unthinkable for any society which is fenced off from the world by impenetrable state frontiers and ideological barriers. A country can develop its full potential by interacting with other societies, yet without giving up its own identity.

"We realized that we could not ensure our country's security without reckoning with the interests of other countries, and that, in our nuclear age, you could not build a safe security system based solely on military means. This prompted us to propose an entirely new concept of global security, which included all aspects of international relations, including the human dimension."

MIKHAIL GORBACHEV, FROM HIS BOOK *MEMOIRS*, EXPLAINING THE REASONING BEHIND THE NEW SOVIET APPROACH TO THE WEST

THE GENEVA SUMMIT

Reagan and Gorbachev were very different individuals. The U.S. president was a former professional actor who had come to politics late in life. By the time of the Geneva summit he was seventy-four years old, and his grasp of policy detail, never strong, was fading. The Soviet leader, by contrast, was a fifty-four-year-old career politician at the height of his powers. This mismatch promised to make negotiations difficult, but in fact a strong rapport developed between the two men, and it played a large part in bringing the Cold War to an end.

SETTING THE SCENE

Both the United States and the Soviet Union began preparing their negotiating positions weeks in advance of the summit. The Soviets, who for economic reasons needed progress on arms control more urgently than the United States, planned to offer some important concessions, including a reduction in the number of SS-20s aimed at Europe from 270 to 243 and a halving of strategic (long-range) warheads. The United States was also ready, in principle, to cut back on intermediate and strategic weapons. An end to the development of the SDI system, however, would simply not be open for discussion.

Mikhail Gorbachev (left) and Ronald Reagan laugh and shake hands at the end of the Geneva summit on November 21, 1985. Both men had good cause to be relieved and even happy at the end of the talks.

SUMMIT SUCCESS

Reagan and Gorbachev met in Geneva on November 19, 1985. The two leaders' first talk, scheduled to last just fifteen minutes, continued for an hour. The meeting was not a particularly friendly one, however, as each man took the opportunity to make frank criticisms of the other's political ideology and foreign policy. At a second meeting later in the day, the inevitable clash over SDI occurred. Then, after a walk outside in the crisp Geneva air, the two leaders returned to their villa for a "fireside chat." This meeting would prove to be a turning point — the two men started to relax and get along.

The summit continued for another day, with Reagan and Gorbachev talking amicably about broad policy issues while their negotiating teams dealt with the details. By the end, the participants issued a joint statement, which declared that they would work to prevent war, nuclear or conventional, between their two countries and would begin new arms control talks. These talks would seek to reduce the nuclear capability of each nation by fifty percent. The Soviets also pledged to withdraw all troops from Afghanistan as soon as it was politically and practically possible to do so.

A NEW RELATIONSHIP

The 1985 Geneva summit led to no binding agreements, except on a few scientific and cultural issues. Yet it altered the superpower relationship on both a personal and a political level. Now the two superpower leaders really wanted to make arms reduction work, and they had committed themselves to a program of action. While huge obstacles still lay in the way of progress — not the least being a continued deadlock on the subject of SDI — a way to overcome them might soon be found.

MIKHAIL SERGEYEVICH GORBACHEV (1931–)

Mikhail Gorbachev was born in Privolnoye, in the southwestern Caucasus region of the Soviet Union. He studied law at Moscow University, and after graduating returned to the Caucasus, where he worked for Komsomol, the communist youth league. Gorbachev rose to become local party chief, and in 1978 he was called to Moscow by the Soviet leadership to take the post of agriculture secretary in the Communist Party's Central Committee. In 1979 Gorbachev joined the Politburo, and in 1985, after the death of Konstantin Chernenko, he became Communist Party general secretary.

In his new role as Soviet leader, Gorbachev revitalized Soviet foreign policy while introducing major reforms at home. His main economic goals were to replace the centrally planned Soviet economy with a semi-market economy and to modernize industry and agriculture. Gorbachev sought to restructure the Communist Party and purge it of corruption, and he tried to establish more democratic elections for officials. He also permitted some movement towards multiparty democracy. In 1990, he was appointed to the new post of president, and that same year he won the Nobel Peace Prize.

Gorbachev was ousted in a coup by hard-line communists in August 1991, and after a brief return to power he resigned on December 25, 1991. He now devotes much of his time to the Gorbachev Foundation, which raises funds for people in need, including Chernobyl victims.

▲ This aerial view of the Chernobyl nuclear power plant shows the extent of the destruction caused by the 1986 explosion.

DISASTER IN CHERNOBYL

On April 26, 1986, staff carrying out tests at the Chernobyl nuclear power plant, in the Ukraine, failed to follow the correct safety procedures. As a result, the plant's reactor exploded and caught fire, sending clouds of radioactive dust into the atmosphere. The wind soon carried this radioactive dust far and wide, contaminating many parts of Europe.

Chernobyl highlighted the economic and political weaknesses of the Soviet Union. The nuclear reactor was out of date, badly designed, and poorly maintained, while Soviet authorities were slow to respond to the explosion and did their best to conceal its magnitude from the outside world. Gorbachev later said the disaster was a turning point for *glasnost*, or openness, because it showed that the lumbering, secretive Soviet government was overdue for reform.

SOVIET INITIATIVES

In January 1986, Gorbachev made an ambitious new proposal to the United States: the Soviets would seek to eliminate all nuclear weapons by the year 2000. He also presented a plan for the withdrawal of all Soviet and U.S. intermediate-range forces from Europe.

U.S. officials believed that Gorbachev's arms reduction plan was too good to be true. The plan did not address the fact that the Soviets had far more conventional forces in Europe than the United States did, and that if each side's nuclear missiles were removed, the Western nations would be at a disadvantage. To the annoyance of his own military, the Soviet leader even offered to shift some troops elsewhere. Yet the offer did not sway U.S. officials, who knew Soviet forces would still outnumber those of the West.

RISING TENSIONS

The Soviets were disappointed by the lack of U.S. enthusiasm for their arms proposals, and two other developments further strained U.S.-Soviet relations. The first was the U.S. decision to increase aid to Afghanistan's Islamic rebels and supply them with Stinger anti-aircraft missiles. By the fall, the rebels were using the weapons to shoot down Soviet helicopters. The second setback occurred on April 15, when U.S. aircraft bombed Soviet-backed Libya, which the United States believed was behind a Berlin nightclub bombing that had killed a U.S. soldier.

THE REYKJAVIK SUMMIT

Despite these and other problems — in August, both the United States and the Soviet Union arrested alleged spies working for the other side — Gorbachev continued to push for another summit. Eventually it was agreed that the Soviet leader would meet President Reagan again in Reykjavik, Iceland.

The meeting, which was held on October 11, 1986, made rapid progress. A proposal to withdraw all intermediate-range weapons was accepted by both sides. Then, after hours of debate, the two leaders agreed to eliminate all nuclear weapons in a decade.

Unfortunately, this breakthrough was not to be. Gorbachev insisted he would confirm the plan only if U.S. development of SDI was confined to the laboratory. Reagan refused, and a vital opportunity slipped away.

VIEWS OF REYKJAVIK

"Believe me, the significance of that meeting at Reykjavik is not that we didn't sign agreements in the end; the significance is that we got as close as we did. The progress we made would've been inconceivable just a few months ago."

PRESIDENT REAGAN, TALKING TO REPORTERS ABOUT THE OUTCOME OF THE REYKJAVIK SUMMIT, OCTOBER 14, 1986

"We have to alter our views on measures connected to the latest hostile behavior by the American administration. The turn of events since Reykjavik reveals that our 'friends' in the United States lack any positive program and are doing everything to increase pressure on us."

MIKHAIL GORBACHEV, AT A POLITBURO MEETING, OCTOBER 22, 1986

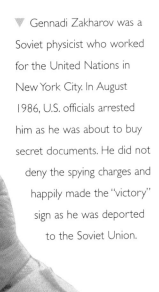

▼ Gennadi Zakharov was a Soviet physicist who worked for the United Nations in New York City. In August 1986, U.S. officials arrested him as he was about to buy secret documents. He did not deny the spying charges and happily made the "victory" sign as he was deported to the Soviet Union.

KEEP TALKING

Despite his frustration over the failed Reykjavik summit, Gorbachev knew that he had no choice but to return to the negotiating table. Without an end to the arms race, his reforms at home could not succeed. President Reagan was also eager to make progress. He wanted to show the public some results from the arms talks, and like Gorbachev he also needed to cut arms spending, which had made a huge dent in the U.S. budget. In 1987, both sides attempted to breathe new life into the arms reduction talks process. Their efforts led to an important breakthrough at the Washington, D.C., summit, which was held in December 1987.

PROGRESS ON INF

Gorbachev made the first move by declaring, in February 1987, that he was ready to go ahead with the withdrawal of intermediate-range nuclear forces (INF), even if the United States refused to budge on the SDI issue. U.S. and Soviet negotiating teams then began to work out the details of the agreement so that it could be signed later in the year. Soviet foreign minister Eduard Shevardnadze and U.S. secretary of state George Shultz also met regularly to solve particularly difficult problems, such as the highly sensitive issue of how each side would verify the other side's destruction of weapons.

BRITAIN AND FRANCE

Unfortunately, Gorbachev's INF proposal would not eliminate all nuclear weapons in Europe. The United States was not the only Western power with nuclear capability — both Britain and France also possessed nuclear weapons. When British prime minister Margaret Thatcher visited Moscow in March 1987, Gorbachev tried to convince her that the elimination of all nuclear weapons was vital, but Thatcher dismissed the idea. French president François Mitterrand shared her view. Both leaders feared that Reagan might return to the Reykjavik summit plan to destroy all U.S. nuclear weapons, and they were determined to maintain their own nuclear deterrents.

THE WASHINGTON SUMMIT

The summit in Washington began on December 7, 1987, and Reagan and Gorbachev signed the INF treaty the next day. In so doing, they set in motion the destruction of a complete class of nuclear weapons — 1,566 Soviet and 846 U.S. intermediate-range missiles. The two leaders also approved comprehensive on-site inspections to verify the process.

The INF treaty was a major milestone for nuclear disarmament. Intermediate-range weapons, however, made up only about three percent of the superpowers' combined nuclear arsenals. Despite the the triumph of the Washington summit, a solution to the larger problem of reducing the two nations' strategic nuclear weapons was still not in sight.

▲ With his wife Raisa by his side, Gorbachev makes a speech to the American people upon arriving in the United States in December 1987.

GORBYMANIA

On December 10, the last day of the Washington summit, Gorbachev and his wife Raisa were making their way through Washington's city streets by limousine. Noticing the crowds that were cheering his progress, the Soviet leader asked his driver to stop, then got out and began greeting the people with handshakes and hugs. This was an experience that he never forgot — the citizens of the Soviet Union were much less appreciative of his efforts to bring about change.

"Gorbymania" was not only evident on the streets. The Soviet leader was also fêted at grand dinners and acclaimed by the media. In 1987, *Time* magazine chose Gorbachev as "Man of the Year."

▲ Some 2,000 Soviet troops in about 300 armored vehicles head for home through a barren Afghan landscape in August 1988.

CHANGE IN MOSCOW

"Quite possibly, we're beginning to take down the barriers of the postwar era; quite possibly, we are entering a new era in history, a time of lasting change in the Soviet Union. We will have to see."

PRESIDENT REAGAN, TALKING ABOUT THE MOSCOW SUMMIT, JUNE 3, 1988

"The Americans did not accept our bold and entirely realistic plan ... directed at ... a decisive transition toward the creation on the continent of a situation of non-offensive structure of arms and armed forces at a considerably reduced level. I believe that a good opportunity has been missed to get things moving, lessening the danger of confrontation between the two most powerful alliances and thus embracing national security."

MIKHAIL GORBACHEV, COMMENTING ON THE U.S. REFUSAL TO ACCEPT HIS PROPOSAL FOR TROOP REDUCTIONS IN EUROPE AT THE MOSCOW SUMMIT

EXIT FROM AFGHANISTAN

In 1986, Gorbachev had described the war in Afghanistan as a "bleeding wound." In February 1988, he finally announced his intention to withdraw Soviet troops. An agreement on the withdrawal process was signed in Geneva, Switzerland, in April, and by February 1989 the Soviet withdrawal had been completed. The conflict between the Islamic rebels and the Afghan government, now headed by Najibullah Ahmadzai, raged on for many years afterwards. Some 20,000 Soviet soldiers had died in vain.

THE MOSCOW SUMMIT

The fourth and final summit between Reagan and Gorbachev, which began in Moscow on May 29, 1988, was more notable for its dramatic setting than for any big arms control breakthroughs. Since the United States refused to make concessions on SDI, progress on strategic weapons seemed unlikely to happen. The two leaders did ratify the 1987 INF treaty. Gorbachev also proposed that members of NATO and the Warsaw Pact — an alliance of Eastern European communist countries and the Soviet Union that was founded in 1955 — should cut back their conventional forces in Europe by a half million troops. The United States was not ready for such a drastic change and rejected the proposal.

The Moscow summit was, however, a public relations triumph. At one point, Reagan and Gorbachev strolled around

Red Square like old friends, providing the perfect photo opportunity. When a journalist asked Reagan if he still thought the Soviet Union was an evil empire, the answer was a firm "no." There could have been no clearer sign that the Cold War was fading fast.

NEW BEGINNINGS

On December 7, 1988, a month after Republican vice president George Bush was elected U.S. president, Gorbachev delivered a dramatic speech at the United Nations in New York City. Over the next two years, he announced, the Soviet Union would cut its forces in Europe by half a million troops, 10,000 tanks, 8,500 pieces of artillery, and 800 aircraft. The Soviet Union, he said, would make the reductions regardless of U.S. reductions. Gorbachev also stressed his commitment to "freedom of choice," implying that countries in Eastern Europe ought to be able to govern themselves as they saw fit.

The United States welcomed this development and President Reagan bade Gorbachev a fond farewell at their final meeting. Many high-ranking members of the Soviet military, however, were upset with Gorbachev's planned reductions in conventional forces. In the future, the Soviet leader's problems would increasingly come from his own people.

▶ Gorbachev makes his groundbreaking speech, in which he announces cuts in Soviet forces, at the United Nations in December 1988.

HUMAN RIGHTS

By 1988, the Soviet Union was making clear progress on human rights issues. Gorbachev had abandoned the Soviet government's long-standing persecution of religious organizations, and in June 1988 the Russian Orthodox Church was able to celebrate publicly the 1000th anniversary of its founding. Two famous Soviet dissidents had already been released in 1986. Anatoly Sharansky, a Russian Jew who had monitored Soviet breaches of the Helsinki Final Act, was allowed to emigrate to Israel. Andrei Sakharov, a physicist and human rights activist, was released from internal exile in the city of Gorky. In 1989, Sakharov became a member of the new Congress of People's Deputies, but died shortly afterwards.

CHAPTER SIX

The Final Years

WHITE HOUSE CAUTION

When George Bush took office as U.S. president in 1989, he put the brakes on the arms reduction process. Bush wanted to make his own assessment of the Soviets and ordered a wide-ranging review of U.S.-Soviet relations. The review concluded that the Soviets could not yet be trusted. Gorbachev had made progress on arms control and domestic policy, but was he just strengthening the Soviet economy before reviving the nuclear threat? Also, who could guarantee he would not be replaced by a more aggressive leader? Bush decided to watch and wait — the United States would be making no new arms concessions in the foreseeable future.

MOVING TOO SLOW?

"[I am] sick and tired of getting beat up day after day for having no vision and letting Gorbachev run the show. This is not just public relations we are involved in. There's real danger in jumping ahead. Can't people see that?"

GEORGE BUSH, REACTING TO COMPLAINTS THAT HE WAS TOO SLOW TO RESPOND TO GORBACHEV'S ARMS REDUCTION PLANS

BUILDING BRIDGES

As time passed, however, the Bush team began to work more closely with the Soviets. Secretary of State James Baker and Soviet foreign minister Eduard Shevardnadze in particular developed a strong relationship. In May 1989 the two met in Moscow, where Baker could plainly see that the Soviet Union was sinking into chaos. It did not look like a country capable

▶ President Bush's secretary of state, James Baker (left), and Soviet foreign minister Eduard Shevardnadze meet for discussions in Moscow in May 1989.

of making a bid for world domination. That same month, Gorbachev announced the removal of 500 more Soviet warheads from Europe.

EASTERN EUROPE

The situation in the Soviet Union and Eastern Europe, meanwhile, was changing at breakneck speed. With his reforms and his 1988 speech on "freedom of choice," Gorbachev had unleashed forces that he simply could not control. Some Eastern European countries began dismantling their old Soviet-controlled governments.

Hungary was the first country to make a move. In January 1989, Hungary's parliament legalized opposition parties and announced democratic elections for 1990. In May, Hungary's border with non-communist Austria was opened and people began to move freely between the two nations.

Poland also experienced change. In April 1989, an accord legalized Solidarity once again and also allowed opposition parties. In the June elections that followed, Solidarity won the majority of votes.

GEORGE HERBERT WALKER BUSH (1924–)

George Bush was born in Connecticut, which his father represented as a U.S. senator. After serving as a navy pilot in World War II, Bush received an economics degree from Yale University. He then moved to Texas to establish an oil-drilling business.

In 1967, Bush was elected to the House of Representatives as a Republican from Texas. In 1970, he became U.S. ambassador to the United Nations, and then, after a brief spell as chairman of the Republican Party National Committee, he was sent to China as President Ford's special envoy. After returning to the United States in 1976, Bush headed the Central Intelligence Agency (CIA), but he was replaced when Jimmy Carter took office in 1977. He was elected U.S. vice president under Ronald Reagan in 1981.

After eight years as vice president, Bush took office as U.S. president in 1989. During the 1988 presidential election campaign, he won widespread support with his slogan "Read my lips — no new taxes." His major achievements as president include continuing a dialogue with the Soviet Union, and thus helping to end the Cold War, and his handling of the Gulf War in 1991. Bush lost the 1992 presidential election to Democrat Bill Clinton.

CHANGE IN CHINA

Since 1985, Gorbachev had tried to reduce tensions between the Soviet Union and China. Finally, in May 1989, he visited the Chinese capital of Beijing with the goal of normalizing relations between the two nations. While there, he witnessed a huge antigovernment demonstration in Beijing's Tiananmen Square. The day after Gorbachev left, the crowds were brutally dispersed by troops. The Soviet Union and Eastern Europe were not the only places where communism faced resistance.

THE PACE OF CHANGE

While the relationship between the United States and the Soviet Union slowly improved in the second half of 1989, the pace of change in Eastern Europe accelerated. One by one, countries that had been under Soviet domination for over forty years threw off communist rule.

CHANGING VIEWS

In July 1989, President Bush went to Poland and Hungary to see for himself the momentous change occurring in those countries. Moved by the genuine enthusiasm for democracy he witnessed, Bush began to reconsider his views about Gorbachev. After the trip, he wrote to the Soviet leader and proposed that they meet. It was eventually agreed that a summit would be held off the coast of Malta later in the year.

Before the Malta summit, Soviet foreign minister Eduard Shevardnadze joined U.S. secretary of state James Baker for talks at Baker's Wyoming ranch. A breakthrough came when Shevardnadze announced that the Soviets would continue START negotiations without any U.S. concessions on SDI.

EASTERN EUROPE ON ITS OWN

"We're not here to make you choose between East and West ... we're not here to poke a stick in the eye of Mr. Gorbachev; just the opposite — [we're here] to encourage the very kind of reforms that he is championing ..."

EXTRACT FROM A SPEECH MADE BY PRESIDENT BUSH DURING HIS VISIT TO POLAND IN JULY 1989

"Any [Soviet] interference in [Eastern European] domestic affairs of any kind, any attempts to limit the sovereignty of states ... is impermissible."

EXTRACT FROM A SPEECH MADE BY GORBACHEV TO THE COUNCIL OF EUROPE ON JULY 6, 1989

FALL OF THE BERLIN WALL

In early October, Gorbachev visited East Germany. Officially called the German Democratic Republic (GDR), the country was celebrating the fortieth anniversary of its formation, which occurred when Germany was divided into a communist eastern side and a democratic western side in 1949. East Germany was led by Erich Honecker, a hard-line communist with little patience for Gorbachev or his reforms. The East Germans, however, were eager for change, as well as for reunification with West Germany.

Gorbachev's visit fueled unrest, and after his departure mass protests erupted.

Honecker was ousted by East German security chief Egon Krenz, who introduced some reforms but could not effectively resist pressure for more change. On November 9, 1989, the government announced that the Berlin Wall, which had sealed off East Berlin from West Berlin since 1961, would open that night. Crowds of people made their way joyfully through crossing points. Others helped dismantle the concrete structure, reducing much of this hated Cold War symbol to rubble.

▲ As crowds watch, a part of the Berlin Wall is removed. In the twenty-eight years of the Berlin Wall's existence, at least eighty people were killed trying to cross it from East Berlin.

BULGARIA AND CZECHOSLOVAKIA

Unrest in Eastern Europe kept spreading. In November, Bulgaria's communist leader, Todor Zhivkov, was overthrown. That same month, the nonviolent "Velvet Revolution" began in Czechoslovakia. The country's communist leader, Milos Jakes, resigned on November 24 after mass protests in Prague, and the constitution was then amended, depriving the communists of their "leading role" in Czech politics. Further protests led to democratic elections in December. Alexander Dubcek, a longtime opponent of the communist regime, became federal assembly chairman, while playwright Vaclav Havel, who had played a major role in the reform movement, became president.

▼ Soon-to-be president Vaclav Havel waves to cheering crowds in the Czech capital of Prague in December 1989. The crowds are celebrating a new democratically elected government.

45

THE MALTA SUMMIT

Although Gorbachev had met Bush when Bush was still vice president under Ronald Reagan, the two-day Malta summit, which was held on ships off the coast of Malta in December 1989, was the first occasion when both men sat down together as heads of state. At that point, Bush was convinced of Soviet good intentions and was ready to negotiate. Gorbachev, struggling to cope with unrest in Eastern Europe and at home, was even more eager to make progress.

THE END OF THE COLD WAR

"We buried the Cold War at the bottom of the Mediterranean Sea."

AN ASSESSMENT OF THE MALTA SUMMIT BY SOVIET FOREIGN MINISTRY SPOKESMAN GENNADY GERASIMOV

ARMS AGENDA

Both leaders wanted to move ahead with START and agreed their teams should prepare a treaty for the next summit, which was scheduled for mid-1990 in Washington. In addition, a conventional forces in Europe (CFE) treaty would likewise be prepared for the next summit.

Developments in Eastern Europe were another important area of discussion. Bush wanted assurances from Gorbachev that the Soviets would not send in troops to revive the communist regimes falling like dominoes across the region. Gorbachev was more than happy to comply. The Brezhnev Doctrine (see sidebar, page 21) was dead and buried.

▼ President Bush and Mikhail Gorbachev aboard the Soviet ship *Maxim Gorky*. It was one of two vessels used for the Malta summit, the other being a U.S. ship, the U.S.S. *Belknap*.

Talks about Central America were less productive. Bush made no effort to hide his anger at the continuing flow of Soviet arms to the region. He was also upset that the Soviet Union had not stopped its communist ally, Cuba, from supplying the Sandinistas in Nicaragua. Gorbachev replied that Cuban leader Fidel Castro did as he pleased, so Bush would have to complain to him directly. The Soviet leader also argued that the United States often intervened elsewhere, so could not criticize others for doing the same.

REBELLION IN ROMANIA

At the end of 1989, Romania joined the ranks of Eastern European countries whose communist regimes had fallen. Dictator Nicolae Ceausescu had ruled Romania with a brutal hand since 1956. In 1989, however, he finally pushed the Romanian people too far when he sent a dissident Protestant priest, Laszlo Tokes, into exile. Although mass street protests began in mid-December, they seemed unlikely to produce any lasting change. Then the army also turned against Ceausescu. He and his wife Elena were tried and shot on Christmas Day.

ECONOMIC ISSUES

A wide range of economic issues was also discussed at the Malta summit. President Bush now believed *perestroika* was genuine and wanted to do all he could to support Gorbachev's implementation of the policy. Bush offered to provide economic advisers who could help the Soviets make the transition to a market economy. He also proposed a new and much more favorable trading agreement between the United States and the Soviet Union.

▼ Nicolae Ceausescu and his wife Elena. Before Ceausescu's death, the terrified Romanian people obeyed his will. For those who dissented, a brutal secret police, the *Securitate*, was always on call.

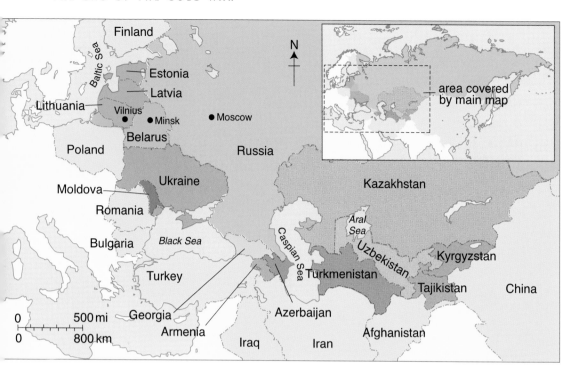

Finland

Baltic Sea

Estonia
Latvia
Lithuania
Vilnius • Minsk
• Moscow

Poland
Belarus

Moldova
Ukraine
Romania

Russia

Kazakhstan

N

area covered
by main map

Bulgaria   Black Sea

Aral
Sea

Uzbekistan

Kyrgyzstan

Turkey
Caspian Sea
Turkmenistan

Tajikistan
China

0   500 mi   Georgia
0   800 km   Armenia
Azerbaijan
Afghanistan

Iraq   Iran

▲ This map shows the borders of the Soviet Union and the fifteen republics that comprised it. All the republics except the Baltic states are now loosely allied in the Commonwealth of Independent States (CIS).

INTERNAL COLLAPSE

In 1945, British prime minister Winston Churchill had called the new divide between communist and democratic Europe an "iron curtain." By 1990, this divide no longer existed, and a major part of the Cold War conflict died along with it. The Soviet Union was now almost alone in pursuing a communist ideology and system of government. As the new decade began, however, not only Soviet communism but the Soviet Union itself became threatened, when several Soviet republics began to demand their independence.

THE SOVIET REPUBLICS

Officially known as the Union of Soviet Socialist Republics (USSR), the Soviet Union was actually made up of fifteen different states. Russia was the dominant state — in 1987, fifty of the fifty-five ministers at the national government level were Russians. Some states accepted Russian rule, but others — such as the Baltic states of Estonia, Latvia, and Lithuania — wanted autonomy. These states watched Eastern Europe cast off Russian dominance, and they stepped up plans to do likewise.

ARMENIA AND AZERBAIJAN

The first major flare-up of 1990 occurred in the southern Soviet republics of Armenia and Azerbaijan. These two states had a dispute over Nagorny Karabakh, a territory that formed part of Muslim Azerbaijan but was also home to many Christian Armenians. Encouraged by Gorbachev's policies, Armenia sought to win its independence from Moscow and also seize Nagorno-Karabakh from Azerbaijan. In January 1990, war broke out between the two states, and Gorbachev was forced to send in Soviet troops.

THE BALTIC STATES

The Baltic states had first begun to demand autonomy in the 1980s, after Gorbachev came to power. Then, in March 1990, Lithuania declared its independence. Gorbachev, who wanted to reform the Soviet Union, not dissolve it, would not tolerate such a move. He ordered Soviet troops to occupy government buildings in the Lithuanian capital, Vilnius, and blocked oil and gas supplies to the state. As a result, the declaration of independence was temporarily suspended in July.

The two other Baltic states still went ahead with their plans. Estonia voted for its independence in March 1990, and Latvia followed in May. Soviet pressure, however, kept these states from actually realizing their goals.

BORIS YELTSIN AND RUSSIA

In Russia, meanwhile, a reforming politician named Boris Yeltsin led the way for even more change. In 1985, Yeltsin had been appointed to a powerful position in the city of Moscow's Communist Party leadership. Two years later, however, Yeltsin was stripped of the position. By 1990 Yeltsin was no longer a member of the Communist Party, and he preached a far different doctrine than Gorbachev. In Yeltsin's view, the Soviet Union could not be saved and would have to be dissolved. When Yeltsin was appointed head of the Russian republic by its new parliament on May 29, 1990, the scene was set for a major clash of wills.

▼ Boris Yeltsin gains support while visiting a collective farm near Moscow, as part of an information tour on agriculture.

49

THE REUNIFICATION OF GERMANY

Since the fall of the Berlin Wall in November 1989, pressure for the reunification of Germany had been mounting. The chancellor of West Germany, Helmut Kohl, was pushing especially hard for progress. The issue, however, was complex and took many months to resolve.

TWO PLUS FOUR

The Soviets and the Western powers had different ideas about the future of Germany. Gorbachev, who had hoped to avoid reunification, wanted any new German state to be neutral. The West wanted it to be a member of NATO and to side firmly with the rest of democratic Europe. Extensive talks would be needed before a united Germany could be achieved.

In February 1990, U.S. secretary of state James Baker suggested holding "two-plus-four" talks that would include East and West Germany, as well as the four countries that jointly occupied Germany at the end of World War II — the United States, the Soviet Union, Britain, and France. The plan was accepted by all involved.

▼ President Gorbachev and West German chancellor Helmut Kohl were already discussing Germany's future when they met in the West German capital of Bonn in June 1989.

MAKING PROGRESS

During the spring of 1990, East and West Germany worked out the details of the reunification process. In May, for example, they signed a treaty establishing economic and monetary unification. At the end of May, Gorbachev and Bush met in the United States, where the Soviet leader reluctantly accepted that the new Germany would join NATO. After more talks in London, Helmut Kohl visited the Soviet Union to meet with Gorbachev.

This meeting proved to be a crucial one. Kohl managed to persuade Gorbachev to abandon Soviet control over East Germany, and in particular to withdraw all Soviet troops. The East Germans were delighted, but hard-line communists in Moscow were appalled — as was Foreign Minister Eduard Shevardnadze, who had barely been consulted on the decision but still had to defend Gorbachev.

Germany was finally reunited on October 3, 1990. In Berlin, Chancellor Kohl proudly waved to the crowds that had gathered to celebrate. The two countries had been divided for forty-one years, however, and the task of making them a single nation again would be a long and difficult one.

TROUBLED TIMES

By late 1990, Gorbachev was in trouble. Demands for independence from Soviet republics threatened to tear the nation apart, and he was criticized by reformers and communist hard-liners alike. He introduced strict measures to control the population, announcing that the army would fire on protesters if attacked. Foreign Minister Shevardnadze resigned in December and warned that the Soviet Union risked becoming a dictatorship.

THE CFE TREATY

At the Malta Summit in 1989, the United States and the Soviet Union agreed to prepare a conventional forces in Europe (CFE) treaty. At a meeting held in Paris on November 19, 1990, this CFE treaty was signed by the two superpowers, as well as twenty other nations. The treaty limited both troops and arms, and was another important sign of improving relations between East and West.

THE NEW GERMANY

"Whether we like it or not, the time will come when a united Germany will be in NATO, if that is its choice. Then, if that is its choice, to some degree and in some form, Germany can work together with the Soviet Union."

MIKHAIL GORBACHEV, SPEAKING AT A PRESS CONFERENCE DURING CHANCELLOR KOHL'S VISIT TO THE SOVIET UNION IN JULY 1990

UNDER PRESSURE

In early 1991, Gorbachev's problems worsened almost daily. The Soviet Union was splintering as one Soviet republic after another made moves towards independence, while the nation's economic decline accelerated. Boris Yeltsin was taking every possible opportunity to stir up opposition to Gorbachev's rule. The Soviet leader was under pressure from every direction.

▼ U.S. troops in Kuwait City, the capital of Kuwait, on February 27, 1991. They are celebrating the swift defeat of Iraqi troops in the Gulf War.

THE GULF WAR

There were also problems abroad. Back in August 1990, the Arab state of Iraq invaded its smaller neighbor Kuwait. The United States protested at once and begun to gather troops in nearby Saudi Arabia. The Soviet Union was unsure which side to support. Should it back the United States, or its old ally Iraq? In the end, it publicly backed the United States.

Soviet support for the United States included voting for a 1990 United Nations resolution on Kuwait. It stated that if Iraqi troops did not leave Kuwait by January 15, 1991, they would be ejected by force. When the deadline arrived, Saddam Hussein, Iraq's leader, ordered his troops to stay. The United States and twenty-seven allies then launched an assault code-named Operation Desert Storm, which began with a series of aerial attacks. The alliance also prepared for a ground war to begin on February 24, 1991.

Before the ground troops arrived, Gorbachev attempted to mediate the conflict between his old and new allies by holding talks with Tariq Aziz, the Iraqi foreign minister. The talks, however, did not bring results, and the allied invasion of Kuwait went ahead. In an operation of textbook precision, Iraq's forces were driven out of Kuwait in a matter of days.

DIFFICULT QUESTIONS

In the Soviet Union, meanwhile, Gorbachev and Yeltsin were still battling each other. Gorbachev was determined to win support for his idea of a reformed Soviet Union, which, he argued, should still have a central government but should also consist of republics that were sovereign and equal. When Gorbachev held a referendum on the issue on March 17, 1991, the results were promising — over seventy-five percent of the population agreed with him. Now all Gorbachev had to do was draft a treaty that incorporated his plans. The Soviet leader, however, would never finish the task.

Unfortunately for Gorbachev, Boris Yeltsin had insisted on placing a second question on the referendum, asking if the Russian republic should have its own president. Seventy percent answered yes. On June 12, 1991, Yeltsin was himself democratically elected president of Russia. Yeltsin was now in an even better position to challenge his rival. While Gorbachev might have been president of the Soviet Union, he had not been elected by a popular vote.

THE WARSAW PACT

The Eastern European Mutual Assistance Pact, or Warsaw Pact as it was commonly known, was a military alliance between the Soviet Union and Eastern European communist states that was founded in 1955. Its purpose was to serve as a counterbalance to NATO, the Western defensive organization established in 1949. In January 1991, Poland, Hungary, and Czechoslovakia announced that, starting in July, they would no longer play any part in the organization. Bulgaria made the same declaration in February, and on March 31, 1991, the alliance essentially ceased to exist. In July it was officially dissolved. Another Cold War institution had disappeared.

END OF THE COLD WAR

By the summer of 1991, little remained of the Cold War. Yet Mikhail Gorbachev, the man who had done the most to bring about its end, was still struggling to keep the Soviet Union together. It was a lost cause.

HELP FROM G7?

The ailing Soviet economy was one of Gorbachev's major concerns. He turned for help to the "G7," which was a group of the world's seven richest nations. At a meeting in London on July 17, 1991, Gorbachev presented G7 representatives with a new economic plan for the USSR. They were not impressed. President Bush had already made clear that there could be no question of U.S. financial aid unless the Soviet Union could show exactly how it intended to turn itself into a market economy. Gorbachev's plan did nothing of the sort, and, to his frustration, his appeal for assistance was rejected.

▼ Holding Russian flags and photographs of Boris Yeltsin, Moscow citizens listen to the Russian president denounce the coup against Gorbachev in August 1991.

START I

There was better news on arms reduction. Gorbachev and Bush signed the START I treaty in Moscow in July 1991. The treaty restricted each of the superpowers to a maximum of 9,000 warheads and bombs and 1,500 delivery vehicles (such as ICBMs, SLBMs, and bomber aircraft). A plan was made for further reductions to follow.

THE AUGUST COUP

Since June, there had been rumors that hard-line communists planned to oust Gorbachev. On August 19, 1991, while the Soviet leader was away from Moscow on a holiday, the hard-liners struck. Tanks rolled into Moscow, radio and television networks were seized, and a state of emergency was imposed. Gorbachev's vice president, Gennady Yanayev, who helped plot the coup, took over as leader.

Boris Yeltsin now took the step that would seal his victory over Gorbachev. Standing on top of a tank outside the "White House," the Russian parliament building, he declared to the gathered crowds that the coup was unconstitutional and should be resisted. Yeltsin's speech was enough to turn the tide firmly against the halfhearted and hesitant leaders of the rebellion. On August 22, Gorbachev was able to return from the Black Sea coast, but Yeltsin was now in control.

▲ Outside the "White House," or Russian parliament building, Boris Yeltsin (holding speech) stands on a Soviet tank while denouncing the coup against Gorbachev. Although Yeltsin criticized Gorbachev's hard-line foes, the Russian president had his own dreams of power.

FROM USSR TO CIS

The failed coup put an end to Gorbachev's dreams of a revived Soviet Union. Realizing how weak the Soviet Union really was, the Baltic states and other Soviet republics finally broke free. On August 24, 1991, Gorbachev resigned as general secretary of the Communist Party, and five days later the operations of the party were suspended.

The Soviet Union was now in limbo. While the individual republics still existed, it was unclear how, or if, they should relate to one another. The problem was solved by Russian president Yeltsin and the leaders of two newly independent republics, Belarus and Ukraine. On December 8, 1991, they met in Minsk, the capital of Belarus, and formally dissolved the Soviet Union. They then established the Commonwealth of Independent States (CIS), a much looser association of republics that was quickly joined by nine others. The three Baltic states, however, chose to remain completely independent.

AN UNCERTAIN END

Gorbachev officially resigned as president of the Soviet Union on December 25, 1991, with a poignant speech. The Soviet flag, with its familiar hammer and sickle, was lowered over the Kremlin for the last time and replaced with the Russian flag. A once mighty nation was dead and the Cold War was over. No one knew what would follow.

THE VANISHING ENEMY

"We have seen our implacable enemy of forty years vaporize before our eyes."

GENERAL COLIN POWELL, CHAIRMAN OF THE JOINT CHIEFS OF STAFF, ON SEPTEMBER 27, 1991

CHAPTER SEVEN

Cold War Legacy

The Vietnam Veterans Memorial in Washington, D.C., is carved with the names of Americans killed or missing in Vietnam. Those who visit the memorial often make rubbings of the names of lost friends and relatives, which they can take home with them.

For forty-five years, the world was in the grip of the Cold War. The Soviet Union, the United States, and other countries caught in the middle of their struggle suffered its effects, while the potential for nuclear holocaust hung over the entire planet. The legacy of this huge conflict is wide-ranging and enduring.

UNITED STATES

If any country has "won" the Cold War, it is the United States. As the self-styled champion of democracy, it has triumphed over communism, and as a world superpower, it has effectively eliminated its only rival. The country was also able to bounce back quickly from budget deficits caused by Cold War military spending ($400 billion per year during the Reagan era). On a personal level, however, the Cold War has left behind a tragic legacy. Some 54,000 U.S. troops died in the Korean War and almost 58,000 were killed in Vietnam. Many thousands more were wounded.

SOVIET UNION

The Soviet Union, on the other hand, clearly lost. It has ceased to exist, and its former republics, including Russia, have struggled to recover from its collapse.

Under Yeltsin and then Vladimir Putin, who succeeded Yeltsin as president in December 1999, Russia has faced many problems. The economy has steadily declined, and many people, including members of the armed forces, are often not paid for months. Russia cannot even afford to maintain its nuclear installations and weapons. Crime has also risen dramatically, as the Russian Mafia exploits the country's weaknesses.

NUCLEAR DISARMAMENT

In the immediate aftermath of the Soviet Union's collapse, the United States and Russia continued to cooperate on arms reduction, and in 1993 the two countries signed the START II treaty. When introduced, the treaty will limit each side to 3,500 nuclear weapons, while all land missiles with multiple warheads will be eliminated. Unfortunately, the breakdown of law and order in Russia is so great that its nuclear weapons are not easily tracked.

EASTERN EUROPE

Many countries in Eastern Europe have become both politically and economically stable since gaining freedom from Soviet-backed communism. In 1994, NATO began a "partnership for peace" initiative that encouraged these nations to cooperate militarily with the West. Some, including Poland, have since joined the alliance, and many hope that Europe will become more secure as a result. In addition, several Eastern European countries have applied to join the European Union.

GERMANY

Like Russia, Germany has had to cope with many problems since the end of the Cold War. Reunification led to severe economic difficulties, including high unemployment that reached 4.27 million in 1996. The country has also witnessed a growth in racism and neo-Nazi activity, which is often directed against Turks and other immigrant workers.

▲ Vladimir Putin, Boris Yeltsin's successor as president of Russia. Before entering politics, Putin was an official in the KGB, the Soviet secret police, then head of the Federal Security Service, a similar Russian institution set up after the collapse of the Soviet Union.

YUGOSLAVIA

Although not a Soviet satellite state, the former Yugoslavia was a relatively stable communist country until the death of its longtime ruler, Marshal Tito, in 1980. After Tito's death, Serbia, Croatia, and the other republics that made up Yugoslavia gradually began to split apart. This split led to a series of bloody civil wars fueled by ethnic and religious hatred, and eventually resulted in the permanent fragmentation of the country.

Historians and other experts argue that one of the few virtues of a communist authoritarian government was that it prevented situations like that in Yugoslavia from developing. Since citizens were often busy contending with government oppression, other conflicts did not surface.

A CHANGING WORLD

In 1990, President Bush claimed that he believed the end of the Cold War would lead to a "new world order." No such order, however, has yet developed to replace the dependable superpower rivalry of the Cold War years. Instead, many countries are struggling to find their place in the unpredictable and often dangerous conditions of the post-Cold War world.

CHINA

Following the collapse of the Soviet Union, China became the world's only major communist power. Many experts believe that the country, with its nuclear capability, booming economy (the result of reforms introduced in the 1980s), and population of well over one billion people, will one day become a superpower equal to the United States.

The leader of North Korea, Kim Jong Il (left), greets the president of South Korea, Kim Dae Jung. The meeting took place in North Korea's capital, Pyongyang, on June 13, 2000, fifty-five years after Korea was split in two.

CUBA, VIETNAM, AND NORTH KOREA

The world's other remaining communist nations are not flourishing. Cuba, still led by Fidel Castro, has suffered greatly from the withdrawal of Soviet troops and the end of Soviet trade subsidies in 1990. Vietnam has also suffered from the loss of Soviet aid, but in recent years has made efforts to draw closer to the United States. In 1994, U.S. embargos on trade with Vietnam were lifted, and in 2000 U.S. president Bill Clinton paid a visit to the country.

North Korea was virtually cut off from the rest of the world during the long and repressive dictatorship of Kim Il Sung. After his death in 1994, he was replaced by his son, Kim Jong Il, who continued similar policies. In 2000, however, the country sought to improve its relations with non-communist South Korea. The countries' two leaders met in the North Korean capital of Pyongyang, and a hundred people from each country were allowed to cross the border briefly to visit relatives.

WAR AND PEACE

The Cold War's end has certainly not removed the existence of "hot war," or conventional fighting. In 1992, sixty-six wars were raging in various parts of the world, and a similar number still rage today. The nuclear threat has also not been eliminated. The combined nuclear arsenals of today still have a destructive power equal to eight million tons of TNT.

Since January 2001, when George W. Bush took office as U.S. president, Cold War tensions have resurfaced. In March 2001, the United States expelled fifty suspected Russian spies, while Russia expelled the same number of suspected U.S. spies. In April, a U.S. spy plane collided with a Chinese fighter plane off the coast of China's Hainan Island and made an emergency landing. China refused to release the plane and its crew immediately, and relations between the world's leading capitalist and communist powers grew strained. Bush also has plans for a National Missile Defense (NMD) system, similar to the SDI system of the 1980s.

Today, the world is still a dangerous place. Ethnic and religious tensions held in check by the Cold War now fuel many conflicts, and terrorism continues to grow. Yet thanks to years of patient arms talks, the threat of a global nuclear war has largely faded into the background.

THE UNITED NATIONS

The work of the United Nations (UN), which was formed in 1945 to help foster peace and cooperation among countries, was often hampered by the pressures of the Cold War. Since the United States and the Soviet Union both belong to the UN's Security Council, each has veto power over all UN decisions. During the Cold War, one country would often use its veto to block proposals from the other country.

Since the end of the Cold War, the UN has become less divided and has also increased its peacekeeping role, sending troops to such troubled areas as the former Yugoslavia, the Middle East, El Salvador, and Angola. The UN still has restrictions, however, that can make it ineffective. UN soldiers only keep the peace, so they cannot intervene to prevent fighting. Their job is mainly to observe and mediate in disputes without using force.

COLD WAR STABILITY

"For all its risk and uncertainties, the Cold War was characterized by a remarkably stable and predictable set of relationships among the great powers."

LAWRENCE EAGLEBURGER, DEPUTY U.S. SECRETARY OF STATE, SEPTEMBER, 1989

Time Line

1972

FEBRUARY 22
U.S. president Nixon
visits China

MAY 26
United States and
Soviet Union sign
SALT I treaty

1973

JANUARY 27
United States signs
treaty ending its
Vietnam involvement

1974

AUGUST 8
President Nixon resigns;
Vice President Gerald
Ford becomes next
U.S. president

1980

JANUARY 23
U.S. president Carter
lays out the Carter
Doctrine in his State
of the Union speech

SEPTEMBER 17
Solidarity (*Solidarnosc*)
trade union is founded
in Poland

1981

DECEMBER 13
Polish prime minister
Jaruzelski declares
martial law

1982

NOVEMBER 12
Yuri Andropov becomes
the new Soviet leader
following the death of
Leonid Brezhnev

NOVEMBER 19–21
Reagan-Gorbachev
summit held in
Geneva, Switzerland

1986

OCTOBER 10–12
Reagan-Gorbachev
summit held in
Reykjavik, Iceland

1987

DECEMBER 7–10
Reagan-Gorbachev summit
held in Washington, D.C.,
where INF treaty is signed
on second day

NOVEMBER 9
Opening of Berlin Wall,
which allows people to
pass freely between
East and West Berlin;
much of the wall is
pulled down

DECEMBER 2–3
Bush-Gorbachev
summit held off
the coast of Malta

1990

MAY 29
Boris Yeltsin appointed
head of Russian republic

MAY 30 TO JUNE 2
Bush-Gorbachev
summit held in
Washington, D.C.

AUGUST 2
Iraq invades Kuwait

OCTOBER 3
East and West Germany
are reunited

1975

AUGUST 1
Helsinki Final
Act signed

1979

JUNE 18
United States and
Soviet Union sign
SALT II treaty

DECEMBER 12
NATO countries approve
of deployment of U.S.

cruise and Pershing II
ballistic missiles
in Europe

DECEMBER 25
Soviet Red Army
invades Afghanistan

NOVEMBER 24
President Ford and
Soviet leader Leonid
Brezhnev agree to the
Vladivostok Accord

1983

MARCH 23
U.S. president Reagan
announces the Strategic
Defense Initiative (SDI)

NOVEMBER 23
Soviets walk out of the
START and INF talks
in Geneva

1984

FEBRUARY 13
Konstantin Chernenko
becomes the new Soviet
leader following the
death of Yuri Andropov

1985

MARCH 11
Mikhail Gorbachev
becomes the new Soviet
leader after the death of
Konstantin Chernenko

1988

MAY 29 TO JUNE 2
Fourth and final
Reagan-Gorbachev
summit held in Moscow

DECEMBER 7
Gorbachev announces
huge Soviet arms cuts
and commitment to
"freedom of choice" in
Eastern Europe

1989

FEBRUARY 15
Last Soviet troops
leave Afghanistan

MAY 15–19
Gorbachev visits Beijing
to normalize relations

between Soviet
Union and China; pro-
democracy protests
take place in Beijing's
Tiananmen Square

1991

JANUARY 15
Operation Desert Storm
begins against Iraq

JUNE 12
Boris Yeltsin elected
president of the
Russian republic

JULY 31
Bush and Gorbachev
sign START I treaty
in Moscow

AUGUST 19
Gorbachev temporarily
ousted by hard-line
communist rebels

DECEMBER 8
Soviet Union is officially
dissolved and the

Commonwealth of
Independent States
(CIS) is established

DECEMBER 25
Mikhail Gorbachev
resigns as president
of the Soviet Union

Glossary

antiballistic missile: missile that can intercept and destroy ballistic missiles.

ballistic missile: missile that reaches the top of its arc with rocket power and then falls freely to its target.

capitalist democracy: an ideology and style of government based on elected, representative leaders, individual liberty and ownership of property, and an open competitive market that determines prices and wages.

colony: territory a country controls in order to exploit its resources.

communism: ideology that advocates government owning all property and controlling the economy in order to create a classless society, and which often involves authoritarian rule.

coup: sudden overthrow of a country's leader or government.

cruise missile: low-flying missile that is powered throughout its flight.

détente: diplomatic term that describes a lessening of tensions and greater understanding between former enemies.

dissident: person who is opposed to a government or other official body.

glasnost: under Soviet leader Gorbachev, policy of increased political openness in the Soviet Union.

ideology: belief or way of thinking, as in communist or capitalist ideology.

martial law: rule that is imposed and enforced by a country's armed forces, usually during a national emergency.

NATO: acronym for North Atlantic Treaty Organization, a defensive alliance of Western nations established in 1949.

perestroika: policy under Soviet leader Gorbachev that sought to restructure the economy of the Soviet Union.

Politburo: name of the main policy-making body of the Soviet Communist Party, and a shortened form of the Russian word for "political bureau."

ratify: to approve officially.

satellite state: country that is controlled by another, more powerful, state.

SDI: acronym for Strategic Defense Initiative, a program proposed by U.S. president Reagan that involved creating a high-tech, space-based weapons system designed to protect the United States from missile attack.

secretary of state: official responsible, under the U.S. president, for conducting U.S. foreign policy.

Security Council: decision-making body of the United Nations, consisting of its five permanent members (China, France, Russia, the United Kingdom, and the United States).

Solidarity: trade union, established in Poland in 1980 with Lech Walesa as its leader, that sought reforms from the communist Polish government.

sovereignty: ability of a state to govern itself without outside intervention.

strategic missile: long-range missile that can hit targets up to 3,400 miles (5,500 km) away.

Warsaw Pact: common name for the Eastern European Mutual Assistance Pact, a military alliance between the Soviet Union and communist states in Eastern Europe that was established in 1955 and dissolved in 1991.

Books

Cold War: An Illustrated History, 1945–1991
Jeremy Isaacs and Taylor Downing
(Oxford University Press)

The Cold War (*Guides to Historic Events
of the Twentieth Century* series)
Katherine A. S. Sibley
(Greenwood Press)

Memoirs Mikhail Gorbachev
(Doubleday)

*Russia, America and the Cold War:
1949–1991* (*Seminar Studies in
History* series) Martin McCauley
(Longman)

Videos

CNN Perspectives Presents: The Cold War
(Turner Home Video)

Biography: Gorbachev
(A & E Entertainment)

The Fall of the Berlin Wall
(Warner Home Video)

*Red Star Rising — The Dawn of the
Gorbachev Era* (MPI Home Video)

Web Sites

Cold War
www.cnn.com/SPECIALS/cold.war

Mikhail Gorbachev
**www.time.com/time/time100/
leaders/profile/gorbachev.html**

The Cold War Museum
www.coldwar.org

Nuclear Files
www.nuclearfiles.org

Index